Mandalas for Healing

Wolfgang Mertl and Hubert Janko

Sterling Publishing Co., Inc.
New York

Library of Congress Cataloging-in-Publication Data available

10   9   8   7   6   5   4   3   2   1

Published by Sterling Publishing Company, Inc.
387 Park Avenue South, New York, N.Y. 10016
Based on a work originally published in Austria
under the title *Die 12 Siegel der Heilung* and
© 2001 by METATRON-Verlag®, A-4863 Seewalchen, Austria
English translation ©2002 by Sterling Publishing Co., Inc.
Distributed in Canada by Sterling Publishing
c/o Canadian Manda Group, One Atlantic Avenue, Suite 105
Toronto, Ontario, Canada M6K 3E7
Distributed in Australia by Capricorn Link (Australia) Pty. Ltd.
P.O. Box 704, Windsor, NSW 2756 Australia

Sterling ISBN 0-8069-8489-9

An Important Note

The application of these healing mandalas in no way can be a substitute for treatment by a doctor or a therapist in cases of medical necessity. If you have persistent physical or psychological problems, please do not hesitate to seek the advice of a professional.

When it comes to serious illnesses, these mandalas play an important role in supporting conventional medical treatment. As a supplementary form of therapy, they help eliminate some of the fundamental causes of illness, which are dissolved in the thoughts, feelings, and attitudes of the person, thus contributing to lasting healing.

If emotional problems are eliminated, or at least lessened substantially, many potential illnesses can be averted in the future. This is because, with inner conflicts, the pressure builds up in the psyche, and then can spill over to the physical level, manifesting as all kinds of symptoms. By changing our thoughts and feelings, however, we can avoid the outbreak of many symptoms and disorders.

Contents

About the Authors

An illustrator and a computer technician, Hubert Janko came up with the idea of creating a book about mandalas that have an effect on human beings, but that go far beyond the centering and relaxation effects already recognized. It was his view that it was possible to create a finely differentiated system whereby mandalas could be used to combat all kinds of illnesses and negative psychic conditions.

Janko found in Wolfgang Mertl the perfect partner. Having been a therapist for many years, Mertl not only had amassed a wealth of knowledge regarding both Eastern and Western holistic healing methods but also about symbols and their effects on the human organism. Thus began the collaboration of Janko and Mertl, which came to fruition in this book of mandalas with special effects on healing body, mind, and spirit.

Wolfgang Mertl was drawn early on to methods of holistic healing, which views the human being in his or her totality. Then he became engaged in the study of traditional Chinese medicine, focusing on acupuncture and acupressure, as well as Chinese healing herbs. In order to integrate the aspects of body, mind, and spirit fully in his own experience, he began, at the same time, an intensive training in Qigong (sometimes transliterated as "Chi Kung"), an ancient Chinese system of meditative physical exercises. This same intention led him to learn diverse medi-

tation techniques, the Feldenkrais therapy method, and yoga, as well as various martial arts with different masters.

Not only was Mertl fascinated by Eastern healing methods, he also saw that the West has a lot to offer regarding knowledge of the body on an energetic level. Delving into this knowledge, he came to recognize an array of complex mental and spiritual associations.

This led him to research different healing systems further, particularly European healing herbs. Then he became interested in the exploration of ancient places of power as well as the energy meridians of the earth, which has contributed astonishing new insights to energetic knowledge.

In addition, he became intensely absorbed in the philosophical aspects of various faiths, including Taoism in the East and Christian mysticism and the Druid teachings in the West. From this, he came to see increasingly that all things are one, that we are connected in a special way with our environment and one another.

Thus, through his own experience and from his work as a therapist, little by little, over the years, Wolfgang Mertl has gleaned a complex system of interconnections with symbolic associations on many different levels in the human organism. The sum of this knowledge provides much of the rich content for Hubert Janko's vision.

Preface

The healing mandalas presented in this book were developed based on the knowledge that specific forms, arranged in special ways and in connection with particular colors, have a definable and targeted effect on human beings.

Initially, this book was going to be focused on achieving immediate help for everyday ailments, temporary weaknesses, and emotional problems, as well as relieving acute pain. Many years of research and gathering of data based on experiences went into the development of this book. In addition, seemingly endless hours of drawing different mandalas and testing their specific effects were necessary to arrive at the final form of the healing mandalas offered on these pages. Finally, it was determined that these special mandalas not only have an effect on physical and emotional levels, but also loosen up blockages and balance weaknesses in character, and even play a role in spiritual development.

The transformative effects of these mandalas were tested and documented empirically as well as clinically. The application of the individual mandalas can be found in the indexes of physical ailments and problems on the level of the psyche, beginning on page 107, as well as in the chapter displaying the mandalas in color, starting on page 37.

With the numerous mandalas presented on these pages, most physical, mental, and emotional problems are covered. These mandalas can be used as first-aid measures in cases of acute pain or emotional distress. You simply place your hand on each mandala that, according to the index, is applicable to your specific problem. Should you have a physical condition diagnosed by a doctor as being chronic, you color the respective mandala instead; you do the same for persistent emotional problems.

When it comes to the realm of the psyche, you will feel more capable of mastering your life situation due to the healing and harmonizing that takes place on a deep level from working with these mandalas. In no time, you will see how strength returns where it once was lacking, how you can handle daily annoyances with greater calmness, or how you are now able to tackle a project that you had postponed forever.

When the blockages and the thinking and behavioral patterns that make us ill are eliminated, nothing stands in our way anymore, and we can experience a sense of inner harmony or a quick recovery from an illness.

Introduction

The word "mandala" stems from Sanskrit, the classical language of India and of Hinduism, and means "circle."

We see mandalas everywhere in life. The iris of the human eye is a mandala. Think of the wheel, the potter's wheel, the face of the clock. When we look at nature, we see the most beautiful mandalas in the rosettes of flowers. In the transverse section of trees, we can recognize mandalas, as we can in the perfect structure of a snowflake. Even in outer space, in our solar system, this configuration is apparent in the orbits of the planets around the sun. Our solar system unites with many others in the Milky Way galaxy, which in its arrangement is a perfect mandala as well. Therefore, we can see that the structural pattern of the mandala exists throughout nature and the entire universe.

Many highly developed cultures have occupied themselves over the course of centuries with the pervasiveness of the circle, and have thus arrived at a deep knowledge about life and human

Church ornament

existence. They were all aware of that which stands behind the form of the mandala, which can be called the *energetic essence of the circle.* This essential form has made a deep impression on the collective human psyche, manifesting across all cultures and religions. Take, for example, such variations as the artistic rosette windows of the large Gothic cathedrals, the floor plans of temples and other holy places, sacred dances, and meditation pictures, most notably Tibetan art.

Throughout history, not only has the mandala been decorative, but it has also been ascribed a strong symbolic meaning, with practical applications. In many cultures, people tried to reach self-realization and bring about healing through meditation on the mandala. At the same time, it was taken for granted that the mandala reflected the inner life of its creator.

Spiraling celestial dust

Floor plan for the Santa Constanza in Rome, circa A.D. 350

Mandalas: History and Effect

What Is the Origin of Healing Mandalas?

The search for an ideally perfect social order, valid for all people, has engaged visionaries for thousands of years; old books and manuscripts have been dusted off and studied in this quest spanning across all cultures.

The fundamental idea was always, if something is supposedly useful and helpful, then it must be so for everyone. Consequently, there must be knowledge that is generally valid and applicable for everybody, independent of nationality, origin, skin color, social rank, gender, and age.

From this, we can deduce that there must be a superior structure that influences all life processes, giving them their direction. In order to explain this, we must look briefly into a few important areas.

The Fundamental Structure of All Things

Let's examine an object, say, a piece of paper. What does this piece of paper consist of? Wood fibers, unless it is made of hemp or other mixed materials. Now, what do these wood fibers consist of? Smaller and smaller fibers—they become so small that at some point we get down to the cell.

Okay, so what is the cell made up of? Molecular chains. These molecular chains, in turn, are composed of individual molecules. What do these molecules consist of? Formations of atoms, composed of individual atoms. All of this is physics, and you can read about it in any elementary physics book.

The point of this whole discussion is that these atoms are not rigid, immovable particles, but turning, rotating formations of energy that never stop moving. Everything is turning, moving, rotating oscillation, or energy. This happens not only in one atom but also in all atoms, meaning in a toenail or in oxygen, in minerals, and so forth. The reason is that these essential building blocks are contained in every material object, be it visible or not. Nothing can exist without these small building blocks of creation.

Everything Is Oscillation as Well as Color

Without hesitation, we can thus assume that everything swings (it has to, because everything that exists is composed of atoms) and moves, from the most massive rock to the air we breathe. Colors, as well, are nothing but oscillation, and are perceived as such by our organs of sight, with the "image" of color only coming about in our brains.

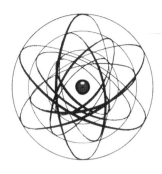

An atom, showing the nucleus with rotating electrons

The fine oscillations trigger impulses in our "switchboard," the brain, which is also the reason why colors evoke reactions in us.

Similarly, each organ in the body has its own specific oscillation. If an organ is weakened or ill, its oscillation deviates from how it was initially. With the right color, however, the organ can regain its harmony.

Now, if we think hard about this and consider what oscillation is, we will realize that oscillation cannot exist by itself. Oscillation alone cannot be the original reason for creation, as there is no oscillation in and of itself.

Every Oscillation Is Caused by a Force

Let's think about how many forces there are. There is the force of fists, the force of a storm, the force of rapid water, for example. Yet, at some point, all of these forces become exhausted. The fist

Condensed matter (white dwarfs)

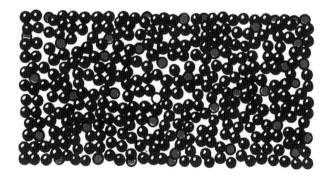

becomes tired, the storm dies down, and water seeps away or evaporates.

If the force in the atom would end, would expire, the atom would dissolve into nothing. As astronomers have proven, it would turn into a "white dwarf," an atom whose distances between its electrons and its nucleus have shrunk to zero. However, this has never happened in the history of the earth. No doubt, there are stars in outer space that, according to the same principle, first were supernovae and then became "white dwarfs," but that is an entirely different story. Thus, this force that keeps the atoms oscillating must have an eternal quality.

Force from Will, Will from Thoughts

According to the laws of nature, there is no force in and of itself. Something that triggers this force and puts it into motion must be behind it. We can call this *will*. Therefore, if matter does not exist intrinsically, but is simply the deceiving expression of concentrated, oscillating energy, meaning it is oscillation, and this oscillation is produced by a force coming from a will, where then does the will come from?

Because a will cannot exist on its own, each will must stem from a thinking, willing intelligence, which we can call *spirit* or *mind*.

Everything that has come about according to the *plan* of evolution is a meaningful, orderly wonderment, which can never originate from itself, because nothing can begin from itself.

As we saw, oscillation cannot exist by itself.

All these wonders, created by spirit, or mind, presume *thoughts,* meaning a deep, world-encompassing thinking from a power that organizes itself as life, or life energy!

It is important to understand that what holds true for the wing of a fly, must—as, after all, everything consists of atoms—also hold true for the entire universe, with its millions upon millions of solar systems, galaxies, suns, and stars.

Thoughts from Only One Spirit

There is only one spirit. Spirit is the origin of all things. Spirit is the highest authority of the universe.

As oscillation and force do not exist on their own, the same can be said for spirit, which is imbued in all of *creation.* And with this, we are at the end—or more appropriately said—at the beginning of all things. We now stand at the throne of that unfathomable, immeasurable entity, both father and mother of all creations, the womb of all things that have ever been and will be. We stand in front of *God,* or however one wants to call this higher power.

As God's spirit exists in every atom, and every form is through God and from God, we can say that God lives in every flower, in every stone, and in every person.

Divine Energy

Throughout the entire universe, there is nothing but God, or this divine force. God is in the smallest creature. God is the beginning and the end of all things that were, are, and will be.

In the *Bhagavad Gita,* a sacred Hindu text, this is written:

If God only for one moment stopped loving the world, all worlds would have to fade away.

This divine energy exists everywhere and influences everything. The Chinese call it "Chi," the Japanese "Ki," the Indians "Prana"; the Greek called this universal force "Energeion," and in the Christian tradition and Christian mysticism it is called the "Holy Ghost." It is self-evident that, no matter by which name it is called, it must make itself visible in a certain form and must have an influence on life.

In the past, such ideas were secret knowledge accessible only to a select group of people—the wise men, priests, monks, and scholars. As human beings consist of more than just the physical body and the intellect, but also of emotions, even back then people from that group of the population turned to the inner dimensions. Then from there, they turned outward to the cosmos, with which the innermost self is intrinsically connected.

The Archetypes and Their Symbols

Finally, the archetypes were discovered. Archetypes are primordial images, impressive forces, and at the same time an important part of our inner world, that influence life. They are elemental "programs" that have existed from the beginning of time, affecting the course of evolution.

These forces and their anchoring in human beings were known to every highly developed culture as well as to all groups of people living in harmony with nature. They are the invisible programs that are responsible for the integrated development of humankind, on physical, emotional, and spiritual levels. The symbols that stand for these elemental forces therefore, in a deep, fundamental sense, are healing.

The Symbols in Connection with the Rhythms of Life

All of us come to a point during the course of our lives where we begin to ask about the meaning of life. Where does the human race come from, what are its roots, and where is it heading? Is there an afterlife? In every highly developed culture and in all groups living close to nature, knowledge about such issues is stored and reflected in everyday life.

Life has always been perceived and lived according to natural rhythms, which are closely intertwined with archetypal phases of development. These archetypal time qualities and energy conditions, bound with all the cycles of nature, influence us in our totality. Everyone and everything has a place in these continuous cycles. Therefore, archetypal symbols are capable of bringing human beings back into the original harmony, to release blockages and to restore the original patterns of oscillation.

Native Americans traditionally have lived at one with nature, seeing it as sacred, and still do in some places today. For Indians (in India), Hinduism has pervaded every aspect of life for centuries. The same is true with Judaism for groups of Orthodox Jews living across the globe. In the Western world, Christianity dominates for the most part, although a scattering of people from all religions—including Jews, Moslems, Buddhists, and Hindus—can be found living throughout Europe and America. Spirituality has many names and faces. Still, that which connects all people, no matter which culture they belong to or in what part of the earth they may have their home, is the striving for transcendence and the *path* there. The stations on this path may appear different from religion to religion, but they are the same at their core.

The Archetypes and Their Connection to Stages of Human Development

These stations on the spiritual path can be equated to archetypes, because they are generally valid for all people in the world to the same degree.

Everybody was born at a certain point in time and at a specific place on this planet. Thus, all of us lie in the sphere of influence of the surrounding planets. Far from wanting to give an astrology lesson here, we simply want to illustrate the cosmic and spiritual developmental path all of us share and the important role that archetypes play in it.

The meaning of the various archetypes that lie behind the symbols actually have little to do with everyday astrology.

The Twelve Archetypal Stages in the Cycle of Human Growth

These archetypes, represented in twelve basic stages of human growth, are the *sacred ground* of humanity. As long as people lived in harmony with the cosmic laws, they were in their prime. Downfall only comes about when the cosmic and spiritual laws are disregarded.

The Egyptians, with their temples, pyramids, and highly spiritual *Book of the Dead*, and the Sumerians, the ancient people of Babylonia, with their poetry about the deities inscribed into clay slabs, testify to the long history of the cosmic and spiritual concerns of humankind. Even Christianity is based on the concept of sacred ground, although throughout millennia people have tried to eradicate this essential idea. The ancient domed cathedrals are constructed according to this essential knowledge, and the symbolism is still visible today; all we have to do is look!

The Celtic Druids of long ago celebrated their seasonal festivities according to special dates that corresponded to cosmic events, the solstices and the equinoxes. They observed the starry sky and felt in themselves the invisible link with time and the changes in nature. Later in this book, we will learn how the specific forms and the time qualities connected to them are deeply rooted in all of humankind.

Therefore, it can be said that these archetypes reflect the most essential ancient knowledge shared by all of humankind.

Only we, in these modern open-minded times, apparently do not need this knowledge anymore, as we have at our disposal the vast array of achievements and techniques of the newest sciences to alleviate our problems. Our ancestors, however, had a completely different orientation. For them, what was most important lay behind the visible world, as they believed that the foundation of all things is God.

If God is the origin of all creation, then human beings come from God. Thus, we are not only mortal beings, but also spirit. Therefore, our very essence, our soul, is immortal.

Why Twelve Stages?

Why are there twelve archetypal stages in the cycle of human development, and not ten? After all, ten is the basis for our number system, and we have ten fingers and ten toes.

For Pythagoras, the great mathematician and philosopher of ancient Greece, the number twelve was sacred. There were twelve tribes of Israel. Jesus had twelve disciples. The cycle of the sun consists of twelve parts, the months, allocated to the twelve constellations of the zodiac in the firmament. In addition, three times four is twelve. The three stands for the trinity; the number four represents the four directions. Therefore, as cosmic order has precedence over human logic, twelve takes its rightful place in the archetypal cycle.

All of us experience certain natural cycles, such as sunrise, sunset, midday, and midnight, and spring, summer, fall, and winter. Although we may call them different names, like "rainy season" instead of "winter," these cycles are universal. Just as nature is cyclic, so too are the different developmental stages of human beings. All of us go through various phases of growth from the beginning of our lives into old age, mentally as well as

The uroboros, a symbol for the circle of life

physically. The first day at school, puberty, the search for a partner, starting a family, work, the so-called midlife crisis, retirement, and finally death—all are important stages in human development. Our spiritual growth, as you will see, runs parallel with these phases.

When we look at the individual archetypal stages—their qualities and their requirements for the unfolding of certain virtues and abilities—we will recognize how strongly we develop in accordance with these archetypes.

The Universal Quality of These Developmental Programs

All of life on earth carries within itself these ancient developmental programs. Therefore, not only is humankind influenced by archetypal cycles, but all of nature is as well. Plants follow specific stages of growth not unlike the archetypal developmental phases of people. There is birth, growth, ripening or maturity, completion, rest, dying off, and again a new beginning. These developmental stages occur in the same succession everywhere, on all planes. This means that no stage can be left out.

These archetypes are universal energy patterns influencing life on all levels.

Everything is under the influence of archetypal patterns, and as long as there is life on earth these patterns cannot be overcome. As we go through these archetypal stages, we are living out the eternal laws of life, the invisible writing of God.

This has nothing to do with astrology (the

The Twelve Archetypal Stages, with Their Symbols, in the Cycle of Eternal Life

1. Birth

2. Growth

3. Blossoming and awakening

4. Knowledge and feeling

5. Strength and maturity

6. Purification

7. Balance and harmony

8. Retreat

9. Longing

10. Will and resurrection

11. Liberation

12. Completion

In this braided pattern, we can recognize the structure of the mandala.

influence of the stars and planets on human affairs), although astrology is also based on the same archetypal forms. Represented by the twelve symbols on the previous page (which you will recognize as the signs of the zodiac), these forms are very old and existed as energetic patterns long before the system of astrology developed. Thus, it can be said that the mandala has a very strong connection to the human energetic resonance field.

The structure and the function of the mandala and the archetypes it symbolizes already existed thousands of years before people tried to foresee the future on the basis of astrological calculations.

The annual rings of trees show clearly in their structure the recurring rhythm of time.

The Meaning of the Twelve Archetypal Stages in the Healing Mandala System

Healing takes effect in multiple ways through the use of these special mandalas. Not only are they healing on a physical-organic level but also on the plane of the emotions, as they have a strong effect on our feelings. What's more, they have a uniquely powerful effect on the spirit, and are thus able to heal spiritual wounds.

By means of coloring or placing your hand on the mandala, the right side of the brain in particular is activated. Thus, the mandalas have an extremely positive effect on inner processes, transforming long-buried unconscious problems, complexes, and neuroses. In addition, many illnesses can be healed, or prevented from developing in the first place, through the elimination of the thought patterns that make us ill.

Before we begin applying the healing mandalas, however, it's important to take a closer look at the individual archetypes as they relate to the twelve stages of development.

The Twelve Archetypal Phases of Development

Phase One:
Birth and Fresh Beginnings

The sun and life on earth are intrinsically intertwined according to the ancient maxim of Hermes Trismegistus: "Below is as above, and above is as below, and everything together is one single miracle."

We know that the sun crosses the equator every year around March 21, signaling the beginning of spring. Birth is the most important process at this time, in the first archetypal phase, when everything pushes toward the light, to the sun.

For human beings, as well, birth is characterized by this first phase. It is also a time of fresh beginnings and initiation. This stage rules over the beginning of a new business or the development of a love relationship. Thus, we can view our entire life as characterized by the archetypes.

All forms of new birth strive toward the light. What is required for this? Strength, to reach the light. Seeds need more and more strength, in order to burst out of the protecting husk.

When a woman brings a baby into this world, she uses all her strength and will in order to endure the birth. The infant needs strength too, striving to get to the light, into life!

Likewise, young plants develop enormous strength, so that they can pierce through the foliage lying moldy on the ground. Roots even burst through slabs of asphalt. The enthusiasm of a new love relationship enables us to defy all odds; the same holds true for the startup of a new business or for every other beginning. It is full speed ahead!

Thoughts of self-assertiveness take precedence over everything else: I want to live, I must live. I am the new, and I will surpass, surmount, and overcome all obstacles!

Phase Two:
Growth

The next life phase after birth must be growth. Nature is the best example of this: After the first seedlings have broken through, it will take only a few weeks until everything is green.

Also for human beings, growth is what follows next. During this phase, the young child grows and develops so rapidly that changes are visible almost daily. This growth, however, is mainly physical, as mental development will come later.

The child experiences its environment with all its senses, thus getting its first impression of the world. This impression, however, is solely material, as mental comprehension is very limited at this stage. Because the child is far from recognizing and applying spiritual truths, it builds a reality

composed of matter and illusion. This illusion has completely taken hold of the child. Living entirely in a material world, the child recognizes no other dimensions of reality.

Growth in a newly established business is characterized by this phase, as long as that growth is purely material.

Our dwelling in just this level of reality should be only temporary. If this lasts longer, we will become subjugated to the material world, and there is the danger of being imprisoned in it our entire life.

People constrained by this limited worldview past the appropriate stage are undoubtedly still young souls (meaning they have a long way to go on the path of their soul's journey). On the other hand, those who are able to see beyond the physical world, pushing open the gate to the blissful divine world, are old souls (having come much closer to the goal of the journey).

People who get stuck in this second phase of egoism and worship of the material world are not the true blessed ones—regardless of how powerful, wealthy, or famous they become—as their world is made up of transient pleasures.

This obsession with material things results in all forms of egomania and greed, and from this arise guilt, suffering, inner emptiness, bondage, dissension (all wars), restlessness, and insecurity. Everyone searches and searches, only to end up in an addiction. When we search for greater and greater gratification on the material level, it is not unusual to become addicted to food, drugs, or alcohol, or even power, money, prestige, or material possessions.

Phase Three: Blossoming and Awakening

The next life phase is the time of sexual maturing, the blossoming into adulthood, or puberty. An awesome mystery is hidden in this blossoming, without which every higher-developed life form would disappear. Lacking the possibilities for procreation contained in this phase, there would be no life on earth as we know it.

In May to June, nature is in full bloom, with the hum and buzz of insects everywhere. The preservation of the species stands in the fore-ground.

Puberty, the stage when we become capable of bearing children, is the expression of this phase on the human biological level. It is the time when the young girl becomes a woman, the boy a man. Young people who beforehand had not paid much attention to the opposite sex now can think of little else. A time of hormonal changes, puberty is a rather stormy life phase, all in all.

On the emotional side, a turning from the "I" to the "you" characterizes this phase of development. For example, the person who before was an egoist will now realize that there are also other people with needs.

Entering the third stage, a person who had been materially oriented will now understand that possessions are not the only things in life that make us happy.

Whereas we were focused solely on ourselves when we were young children, we now open up to others in this third phase of life. Young people in love will put up with many difficulties in order

to be close to their sweetheart. They don't care whether the weather is nice or rainy. They realize that there is more to life than simply going to school, eating, sleeping, or playing. These are the boys and girls who are sitting in school with an absentminded look on their faces and are completely somewhere else with their thoughts.

This phase also has to do with mental and spiritual awakening, which is connected with the soul and the heart. You can be any age to enter this stage—for example, in the prime of your professional life, say, around age forty, or retired, at seventy. Regardless of how old you are, if you were previously fixated on the material world, and now something inside of you has begun to stir, making you realize there must be more, you have progressed to this third stage.

Just as the young person blossoming in puberty is drawn to love, when there is an awakening of the soul we turn to spiritual matters. We have the sense that there must be a level of reality beyond the tangible world. With this awareness often comes the view of a sharp division between a purely spiritual and a purely material world. (In reality, though, there is no separation.) This view of two diametrically opposed worlds frequently causes enormous inner turmoil.

The awakening of the soul characterizes this developmental stage, whenever it may occur in the life of a person.

Without this sense of a spiritual world, there can be no progress in spiritual development—that is, in recognizing and manifesting transcendent values.

The tragedy of this phase, however, is that we often cannot remain in the heights of spiritual recognition. The material world, which held us captive for so long, unrelentingly pulls us back. The person newly in love comes back to reality after the first real fight. Similarly, the person engrossed in his or her career who has a spiritual insight will undoubtedly be enticed back to the material world by the pull of his or her professional life.

Nevertheless, the experience of this phase of awakening is the first and most important step in the recognition of the spiritual. And this first inkling of another realm will remain with us forever.

When it comes to young people, they often entrench themselves deeper and deeper in the material world. This is fine for them, as their time for greater heights will come later. The problem only arises with older people when they suppress this sense of something beyond material reality. Then, there is the danger of getting caught up in the mania of the material world, at the expense of the higher strivings of the spirit.

Why does this happen? The spiritual world wants to be discovered, perceived, and experienced. If there is only a premonition as to the existence of this world, however, rough reality will easily overshadow the splinters of light coming from this direction.

In the past, there were rituals that prepared young men and women for this new life phase, such as rites of passage at puberty. Such ceremonies are important in order to tune the soul into a new developmental stage.

Phase Four:
Knowledge and Feeling

As we progress from awakening to more certainty, we enter stage four, a time typified by knowledge and feeling.

In the yearly cycle, stage four occurs around June and July, when the sun is strong. In nature, this is a time of fertilization and pollination. Male and female forces are drawn to each other.

This unfolding of strength is taking place in human beings as well. Through college studies, our education is completed. We know what we want, establishing foundations in life. We find our partner for life, at least ideally. Puberty, which characterized the previous stage, is now superseded by procreation, meaning that a family is started.

On the spiritual level, the sense of a higher reality is replaced by a feeling of greater conviction, but just in people who already have this type of orientation.

Unfortunately, this sense of a spiritual realm, this tender blossoming of the soul in the previous phase, is soon covered up and suffocated by the material focus of most people's lives, in college and in the following years of building a foundation for their existence. Unnoticed, the material world, this deceptive mania, places a veil over the eyes of young adults, mercilessly blinding them to anything transcendent.

Ideals, and with them the fathoming of a spiritual world and a transcendent basis of all creation, become superseded by more practical concerns. Business, ambition, accumulating possessions, and worry about security (the condition of one's bank account) now take precedence. So, not only do many of these young people fail to manifest the greater spiritual certainty associated with the fourth stage, but they actually regress back to the second stage, where the material world was the only reality. Sadly, many people are imprisoned there all their lives.

For the individual who is drawn to the spiritual world and its beauty, so that the sense of a higher reality awakened in the third stage is not suppressed, there is an acceleration of the spiritual quest. Pushing unremittingly from a position of possibility to a place of knowledge, he or she pursues the mystery of life. Looking at plants, animals, and people, this person urgently asks, "What is the meaning of existence?" and "Where do we come from?" Other questions soon follow, such as "How did the world come into being?" and "Who am I?" as well as "Where am I going—what is my life path?" In search of the answers, he or she embarks on a spiritual quest and a journey toward self-realization.

Paradoxically, in this search, death can be a gateway to the essence of life. When we see a dead animal, or a dead person, lying stiff and rigid, devoid of spirit, it is clear that something that is invisible is gone. In trying to understand what has happened, we can say that the heart muscle burst, the brain stopped working, and so forth. But who allowed the heart to work in the first place? Who created the brain? For that matter, who allows the embryo to grow in the mother's womb? Who tells an apple or pear tree what its leaf and its fruit must be like? How does the bee know that it must stick the pollen into the little baskets at its hind legs? Likewise, who tells the white blood corpuscles to take on their job as health police?

Science has terms for all of this: species memory and gene instinct. But who is responsible for programming our species memory? And how can anything be without some underlying reason or cause?

Many people on the spiritual path come to realize that there is only one force that creates all these miracles: God, or the original spirit, the life force that organizes itself, or however one wants to call this higher power.

In Christianity, Jesus preached essentially God's pure love. Regardless of our religion (or lack of religion), this Christ consciousness is a force that flows in all of us, only waiting to be awakened.

Just as the seasons progress through the year, with summer turning into fall and then winter and spring, humankind continues to develop according to cycles. What is called for in these times, however, is a turning away from the emphasis on linear and technical development toward greater energetic and spiritual growth.

Phase Five: Strength and Maturity

From July to August, the sun is at its zenith, radiating the abundance of its fire power onto the earth.

The main issue for the plant world at this time is the formation of fruit and seeds. As in the previous stage when the goal was fertilization and pollination, the aim now is the activation of all forces so that the fruit can best develop. It is now the heart of the summer, the high point in the cycle of the year.

Translated into human terms, this is the time when all forces are deployed. All of our strength now unfolds in material life. Whether due to the rush of blood or hormone distribution, our strength is also at its peak physically.

On the cosmic and spiritual level, the archetypal fifth stage of human development corresponds to the fifth sign of the zodiac, to Leo, the lion. In astrology, the sun rules Leo, which is a fire sign. Those born under the sign of Leo, according to astrology, are usually warm-hearted, generous, and protective.

In the human life process, however, only the person who has fulfilled the spiritual conditions of the fourth and fifth archetypal phases can be regarded as a Leo, this natural leader. Anyone who, in the fourth stage of knowledge and feeling, has come to the realization that matter doesn't truly exist, but is merely a manifestation of the spiritual world, is free from the delusions of the world. In casting off these illusions, probably after much internal struggle, this person has now acquired the strength and maturity associated with the fifth stage.

What is the spiritual task of this fifth stage? In the first two stages, we are asleep in regard to any spiritual recognition and completely captivated by the material world. In the third stage, the soul awakens to the possibility of a higher realm, which leads in the fourth stage to the recognition that God (or spirit) alone exists. When we have realized that there is only one origin of all of life, meaning God (or any way you perceive this higher power), and when we see ourselves as part of God, there can be just one task for us: to live in such a way that we prove ourselves worthy of this divine connection. Not only must we prove ourselves

worthy to ourselves but also to other people and the environment, to nature.

It doesn't help to know about higher values if we still remain torn by the passions and the temptations of the material world. We must put our knowledge regarding love and harmony into action. We must live the strength of our spiritual convictions; we must become true Leos.

It is important not to fight or suppress our blockages and problems.

This doesn't mean that we should rest on our laurels and not strive to improve. We must all try daily to give our best. However, negative tendencies must never be suppressed; otherwise, they will occupy our thoughts and eventually show up in our lives in one way or another. We need to process negative tendencies, in order to be freed of them. Confrontation, not suppression, must take place. For this process, we need recognition, as well as will and practice.

Unfortunately, most people don't know how to process and overcome these blockages, complexes, and unconscious destructive inclinations (such as selfishness, greed, pride, cynicism, arrogance, and fanaticism). However, the special mandalas in this book, based on the twelve archetypal phases, create possibilities for processing these problems.

Phase Six: Purification

The sixth stage in the cycle of the year comes about in late August and lasts into September. This is the time when the sun loses strength, and this weakening is also visible in nature. Along with less growth in vegetation, calmness settles in over the land. For human beings, this means more time for reflection.

Similarly, at this stage in the human life cycle, our life force becomes weaker. Our driving force is no longer distinguished by blazing flames but rather by a calm, steady burning. This stage normally lasts from about age forty-two to the fiftieth year of our life. At around forty-two, we realize we are not the same as we were at twenty-five or even thirty. We have reached midlife. We stand at the mountaintop of our lives, but we are not at the peak of our strength anymore. From this point, physically, for the majority of people, it is a downhill journey. When we get older, the first physical problems start to show up, sometimes even when we are mindful on many different levels.

In this stage of purification, we need to ask ourselves when we become ill what the meaning of the illness is, what mental and spiritual causes there are for the illness. The way we answer this question will guide us in what we can do to become healthy again.

We are often responsible ourselves for getting sick, although genetics and other factors also play a role. Getting sick frequently indicates that our thinking, feeling, actions, or nutrition in some way or another is out of balance.

Every illness can be seen as some kind of disagreement or quarrel with God—that is, a falling out of harmony into disharmony, or a losing of the harmony with the eternal. Thus, it follows that if we were totally in harmony with God, we would not become ill.

So, not only is right nutrition decisive for this sixth life phase, but also right thinking, right feeling, and right actions. Purification is on the agenda, a leaving behind of old patterns and bad habits.

People who attend to their cars with utmost care, getting them serviced and washed often, are frequently clueless when it comes to taking care of their own bodies. They treat this miraculous interplay of biological forces with a lack of consideration that is incomprehensible, and the consequences are inevitable.

Anyone who wants to enter the second half of life healthily must take on the task of purification, characteristic of this life phase. It is crucial not to wait until you are stricken by an illness to do so.

Conscious nutrition is essential for keeping healthy. How big a role do sugar, white flour, preservatives, and dyes, as well as red meat, alcohol, nicotine, and coffee play in your life? How indispensable are they to you, when you consider their risk to your health, especially when consumed in large quantities? Eating according to what each season offers, not overeating, and consciously chewing and enjoying nutritious food have enormous consequences for us mentally as well as physically.

At school, we learn all kinds of dates and facts, but for the most elementary things concerning our own bodies and well-being, there is obviously not much of a budget. If we are indebted to any teachers at all, it is to those few who passed on knowledge in this regard. It is hard to believe that there is so little interest on the part of educators and others in positions of responsibility when it comes to health.

Phase Seven:
Harmony and Balance

Now that the summer is over, the strength of the sun has diminished a great deal and a calmness pervades all of nature. The last fruits are harvested, as nature has fulfilled its task in this seventh phase. At the same time, the seeds are maturing, so that next year everything can bud again. From September into October, there is balance in nature.

Human beings are in harmony, as well, in this phase of the life cycle. The turbulence of life experienced before gives way to an inner balance. Upon approaching retirement, we don't see things quite so narrowly anymore. A problem only arises when we refuse to slow down, continuing to work until we literally drop dead. Although work is important, if it turns into an addiction it can result in illness. Stress, overexertion of the nerves, and inner and outer restlessness often lead to heart and circulation disorders—the logical consequence of constant tension.

Normally, however, harmony and balance characterize this seventh stage in human development.

Phase Eight:
Retreat

From late October through November, the sun is at a low point. Fall storms rage over the land. Life retreats into the roots, into the earth. This retreat phase symbolizes death, as life is approaching its end.

Nature now comes to a standstill, with the

life juices retreating and the winter slowly beginning its reign. This death is nothing final, but only the sheltering calm until new life awakens.

Something similar happens when we actually die, or at least this is one belief: We retreat into the sheltering calm of the heavens, only to emerge in a new life. When viewed this way, this phase is only a change, a preparation for a new birth.

This retreat finds expression in human biology. The body becomes less and less able to perform. Women now reach menopause, when the production of estrogen ceases and they are no longer able to get pregnant. The biological life phase of old age begins.

Characteristic of the eighth phase, however, is a lack of acceptance of this ebbing and decline. This is a time of major turmoil for many people. Once more, men experience a stirring of sexuality, and they want to prove themselves and show their manly power.

The man experiences a "second spring" before his libido takes a dive.

This stirring of sexuality was supported by mother nature in the third and fourth stages. But now, in the eighth phase, without that support, it causes many men only worry and grief. Therefore, this phase could also be called one of death and sorrow.

We want to emphasize again that the stages in human development have nothing to do with conventional astrology. Therefore, there is no reason to assume that a person who was born at the beginning of October, meaning a Libra, lives only in harmony and balance. Here, the phases of growth pertain to the physical, mental, emotional, and spiritual development of all human beings, regardless of which astrological sign they were born under, as well as independent of culture, nationality, skin color, and rank in society.

The eighth phase also finds expression as an analogy in the Bible, when we look at the expulsion from paradise. Adam and Eve were living in the Garden of Eden. They were happy, because they were at one with God. Although they were naked, they had no shame, being innocent children of God.

This passage depicts an allegory, and it must be interpreted that way to be truly understood. The human being, at that time, was enlightened to the highest degree and united with God. Connected with this are power, freedom, dignity, and the certainty of being in God's image.

As the story goes, there were two trees: the tree of life (the spiritual world) and the tree of recognition of good and evil (the material world). These polar forces symbolize the duality, or the world of appearances.

Now, the apple appears as fruit from the tree of recognition of good and evil, meaning the fruit of sexuality, and the snake as tempter, as driving force and as Kundalini energy. (In Indian sacred healing writings, the Kundalini Shakti is depicted as a rolled-up snake that rests at the base of the spine). As described in the Bible, the snake offers the temptation of a bite of the forbidden fruit, the apple, leading to the awakening of the sexual force. Now, instead of eating from the tree of life and finding knowledge of the spiritual world, the once highly evolved person is lured to taste the apple from the tree of recognition (this stands for consumption and materialism). In essence, we

humans discovered our sexuality. Instead of continuing to live solely on light and God's mercy, we fell from the most elevated spiritual heights to the lowest level of the material world.

"But then their eyes were opened, and they realized that they were naked."

GEN. 3,7

This "fall of man" typifies what can happen in our retreat phase, this eighth life stage. In fact, all disasters in the world can be traced back to the fall of man.

The saddest part is that the fall of man, meaning life that is entirely focused on the material, characterizes life for most people. Instead of the true spiritual love for everything that lives, there is a focus on sex. Of course, sexuality is very important, but only when expressed harmoniously, in love, and in the light.

The focus on sex here, however, stands for something broader: purely material greed and lust, which is bound with satisfaction on the level of the ego. This preoccupation can express itself in all kinds of blockages, manifesting as heightened materialism, exaggerated consumption, hunger for power, aggression, and so on.

Perhaps it pleased the creative power to place this stage as a touchstone and death realm between the earthly and the spiritual worlds.

The gate to the spiritual world, to God's empire, is open only to the person who passes the test of this stage victoriously, overcoming the "poison" of the Scorpio (also the corresponding astrological sign, for those born from October 24 through November 22).

The painting, *The Last Supper,* by Leonardo da Vinci, can be interpreted symbolically along these lines. The twelve disciples represent the twelve archetypes, and Christ stands for the sun. The twelve disciples may also represent Christ's visible body. He himself is the divine spirit of this body. In addition, each body part of the human being can be viewed as corresponding to each disciple (or archetype).

Phase Nine: Longing

In nature, this ninth phase is a time of calmness, as the fields are empty and the gardens bare. Everything lies as if dead and buried. It is late autumn, and winter nears. Now the days are short and the evenings long, and we yearn for the light and the sun.

The drawn-out evenings invite reflection. During this phase, we should grant ourselves more rest and think about life.

It is a time of waiting and of stillness. Not surprisingly, it is also the time of the Advent and Christmas. "Advent," in fact, means a "coming" or "approach." What are the people waiting for? For the resurrection of the light! Just as the soul of the religious person longs in these weeks of the Sagittarius month for spiritual devotion, the body and mind yearn for sun, light, and warmth. Therefore, longing for the spiritual and for light and warmth are in the forefront of this ninth stage of human development.

This is also the stage when we enter retirement. Our libido dies down slowly but surely. The spiritual concerns, which were placed last because

of the job, can now be fulfilled. We reflect more and more about life, what it is all about, how it will go on. We tend to become quieter and to retreat more into ourselves.

This is also a time of spiritual longing, despite the grip of the material world. There is no danger in the material world itself, but in its power over us, as this keeps us away from the realm of light and purity.

It is not the wine that is bad, not the jewelry, and certainly not the beautiful body of a young woman or man. Our attitude is the decisive factor. Whereas one person sees the woman or the man and takes delight in this beauty, another becomes sick with lust and desire. Likewise, one person admires a piece of jewelry, calmly enjoying the sight, but the other cannot rest until he or she owns it.

In the ninth stage, however, we feel a longing to disengage ourselves from the glittering enticements of this world, as we are drawn to the light of purity.

Phase Ten:
Will and Resurrection

Now, in December and January, we are two stages away from the last phase of the yearly cycle. Death and dying are no longer in the forefront, as they were in the two previous stages, but wintry gaiety lies over the land. In deep winter, snow and ice reign.

Midwinter festivals take place: Not the sun's birth, but rather the resurrection of the sun, is celebrated at this time around the world. The beginning of spring, around March 21, when the sun crosses the equator, marks the birth of the sun.

Then the days become longer than the nights. Around December 21, the days stop becoming shorter, and start to get longer, which does not indicate a visible birth, but a turn of the sun. Therefore, the winter solstice is the point of the invisible, but cosmically calculable, resurrection of the sun. This start of the solar year is a celebration of light and the rebirth of the sun, and thus spiritually the resurrection of the spirit.

We can say that winter is the coffin. Who lies in the coffin? Someone who has died. Who was that? The person filled with light, killed by the eighth life phase of retreat. What is spring? Birth, something new. Thus, resurrection is the meaning of this tenth phase.

Now, the last fight begins; this is the fight of the Capricorn, who, mustering all the forces of will, tries to overcome imprisonment in the material world, to be free forever.

In the life cycle, similar things occur from around age sixty-three to seventy. Now we gradually free ourselves from the ties of the physical world: This is the time of retirement, a further decrease of sexual energy, and going inside. Moreover, the person who had little interest in philosophic or spiritual matters gradually begins to reflect on the meaning of life.

Phase Eleven:
Liberation

This phase lasts from the end of January until February. The sun becomes a little warmer, as do the days, although it is still winter.

On February 2, certain Christians celebrate

Candlemas, a festival in honor of the presentation of the infant Christ in the temple and the purification of the Virgin Mary. A holiday taken over from the Druids, it was then called "Imbole," and had to do with preparation for the birth of the sun, which takes place around March 21, marking the arrival of spring.

From the beginning of this phase until the end of June, in certain cultures long ago, this was the time when the people were allowed to marry, as the sun is now gaining strength. Today, there are still a number of dances and celebrations during this time of year, many involving looking for a mate. We know from ancient writings that our ancestors had an innate feeling for the "right time." They also perceived emanations from a person to whom they were either drawn or not attracted. They did not let themselves become swayed by superficialities like a beautiful face or a well-built body; instead, they paid attention to whether their energies were harmonious together or not. Nowadays, it seems that many people choose a partner mostly for external reasons.

In the life cycle, at age seventy to seventy-seven, we free ourselves in this eleventh stage from all worldly attachments. Even if we are still vigorous, optimistic, and healthy, we tend to reflect more and more about death and the hereafter. On the other hand, those people stuck in the first or second developmental stage in their seventies will understand little, as they unconsciously drift toward death.

Whether conscious or not, the transition from worldly interests to concerns more eternal seemingly happens by itself. This is so even for people who have been bound to the material world all

their lives. As they gradually approach the end of life, they find themselves facing the mysterious world of the hereafter, from which they came and to which they will go again. And, as they stand opposite this world, they are pulled to it more and more.

Faced with the true origin of things, they see the pretence of the material world. Realizing that they cannot take anything with them into this other world—not their possessions, not their profession, not even their prestige—they come to see everything connected to the material domain as immaterial dust for this other world.

In this phase, we are liberated from our attachment to the physical world, being drawn increasingly to divine love and light.

Phase Twelve: Completion

The approach of spring lasts from mid-February until March 21. In nature, as well as in human beings (on physical, mental, and spiritual levels), this is the stage of completion; the circle closes.

In the tenth stage of the life cycle—that is, when we are about age sixty to seventy—we see how the life force and our attachment to life have started to wane. In the eleventh stage, the life force and the threads that tie us to the physical world have weakened to such an extent that we finally stand free and unattached, and can go.

Of course, there are exceptions, as many people in this stage cling desperately to life. For them, undoubtedly the physical death that takes

place during this twelfth stage is the end. They cannot imagine a life after death or any continuation of learning after death in other dimensions.

Therefore, they cling with all their might to the earthly world, with all its enticements. It is fear above everything else that rules most people, and the fear of death is the biggest fear we have.

Why? Probably the major reason is that we haven't learned to recognize the spiritual dimension and to live according to it.

Some people believe that, at the moment of death, the divine spirit detaches itself from the physical body, leaving the body an empty, immobile vessel. Not so the spirit, however. The spirit suddenly realizes that there is no death, only a transition. Now with a body of fine substance, the spirit can move freely in the astral world. From this level, the spirit views its life in its entirety, the mistakes as well as the parts infused with light.

Of course, many people believe this earthly life is all there is. For them, everything is a creation of nature, at best. They do not believe in the soul or in a higher power. However, at this point in the life cycle, a turning to the Divine is helpful, in order to make this transition as good as possible.

Mandalas for Well-being and Healing

Reestablishing Harmony in Everyday Life

Having learned about the meaning of the archetypes in the twelve stages of human development, we will now look at their effects on balancing and healing by means of their representation in the mandalas.

The various mandalas, which create through the archetypes a connection to different aspects of life, have the power to loosen blockages on many different levels. Moreover, in conjunction with certain colors, these healing mandalas have the effect of balancing a lack of energy and of reestablishing a harmonious condition. Later, you will learn which precise effects the individual mandalas, based on the twelve archetypal phases, have on us physically, energetically, cognitively, and emotionally, and which patterns and blockages can be released.

At this point, we want to emphasize again that, in order to get the desired effect, the healing mandalas have to be colored exactly in the combinations and colors specified. The colored mandalas recommended in the indexes for the respective problems serve as examples.

Therefore, if you are dealing with a specific illness or physical weakness or any type of negative emotional condition, you need to color the respective mandala following the colored pattern in the book, in order to reestablish a state of harmony. (Of course, in cases of serious ailments or illnesses, a diagnosis by a doctor is necessary.)

Effect of the Colors

In the various archetypes, the individual colors have different meanings. These mandalas are put together in a balanced manner, and they have been tested in practice in regard to their effect. Certain shapes, in combination with specific colors, in special arrangements, result in a mandala that evokes precise effects in human beings and triggers processes of healing.

Pick out the mandala that appeals to you the most from the indexes, according to the mandala numbers or the names of the mandalas next to the problem you want to work on; then make a Xerox copy of the respective (uncolored) pattern in the book, in order to color it according to the colors in the corresponding colored pattern. Crayons or colored pencils work well for this.

> **Note:** Do not use any colors other than those specified for the respective pattern. For instance, if you are supposed to use pink and green, don't use, say, pink and violet, as this would create a different effect, and not the necessarily the one you want.

All aspects of these mandalas are purposeful. If you changed only one small factor, the mandala would have a different effect on you.

To this end, please note the indexes of physical ailments and problems on the level of the psyche, and the healing mandalas recommended for them, beginning on page 107.

Importance of Attention and Intention

If you work hard at the computer, or if you have a lot of stress and pressure in your life for any reason, you can benefit from these mandalas. Each of the mandalas in this book has an effect on many levels. The effect can show immediately or after

> **Tip:** Make a little test. Sense intuitively which mandala is best suited for you. Allow the colors and the shapes to take effect on you. Move your hands over the surface of the different mandalas, and let your senses tell you which healing mandala you need at the moment. When you think you have found the right one, read the text that accompanies it. You will be stunned to what degree your inner voice, your intuitive feeling, is on the mark.

some days, as long as you are willing to enter this process with attention and intention.

Allow yourself time for this procedure, and try to create a state of inner calmness. It's best to work with these mandalas without any outside disturbances or stimuli. This means no music or TV. You need to be able to focus your attention on the mandala at hand and on what you want to achieve.

Application of the Mandalas

In applying the healing mandalas, you need to color in the black-and-white patterns with the specified colors with a degree of force, covering all surfaces, as well as place your hands over them several times a day. Another possibility is to hang the picture, once completed, on the wall or anywhere you are sure to see it (door, refrigerator, next to your bed). This way, the oscillations of shape and color are bound to resonate in your consciousness, which will lead to actual changes in your life.

You can also use the colorful healing and well-being mandalas in the book as objects for meditation. Place your hand daily for three to five minutes onto these mandalas, or onto the mandalas that you colored yourself. Gaze at the circular patterns, letting the colors and the shapes affect

you. As you do this, allow any images, ideas, or inspirations to arise. Maybe you will even hear a sound. People have placed calming mandalas under the pillows of small children and babies. The excellent results of this method have been confirmed over and over.

It is possible to develop a dislike for a certain mandala. This occurs when our unconscious feelings, blockages, and disorders are trying to defend themselves against a healing change. Don't let yourself be disturbed by such a reaction. This is only a sign that you are on the right track. The dislike will disappear after a while, and your sense of well-being will increase steadily.

Use Before Sleep

In cases of illness and routine emotional problems, mandalas are especially successful when used before going to sleep. All nonactivating mandalas are suitable for this. Place your hand on the colorful mandala in the book or on the one you colored yourself, which you can laminate. (Mandalas 1a and 4a most of the time bring about an effect in just five minutes, and they are helpful aids in inducing calm sleep.)

In the phase when we are falling asleep, and during the nightly regeneration phase, when no other stimuli affect us, these mandalas are particularly effective. The chakras in the hands perceive the oscillations of the mandalas, which are passed on through the meridian system, so that they evoke in the sleeping phase the desired effect in the person, beginning a process of healing and harmonization.

Quick Results

After working with the healing mandalas daily for a while (anywhere from a few days to a couple of months), you will notice that certain problems have disappeared from your life. A tangible improvement in chronic conditions after a short time is not unusual. After all, that is exactly what these well-being and healing mandalas are supposed to achieve. In fact, fears and weaknesses disappear most of the time ten to fifteen minutes after placing the hand onto the respective mandala.

Experience shows that children in particular react quite positively in a very short time to the therapy mandalas. School stress, hyperactivity, and neuroses that begin in childhood can develop into big problems later. The therapy mandalas can help lessen these problems before they become full-blown.

As effective as these mandalas are as first-aid measures for alleviating pain, they cannot be a substitute for the possibly necessary visit to the dentist or the doctor. The mandala is not able to remove cavities in teeth. A filling that came out must be replaced. The mandala can be used successfully as a bridge in time, however, freeing you of pain until your appointment with the dentist.

In Cases of Acute Pain

We noticed again and again that acute pain, as in headaches or toothaches, disappeared in only five to ten minutes after having used the respective healing mandala. Most of the time, it was sufficient to leave the hand briefly on the colored mandala listed for that problem in the index. (Often it wasn't even necessary to spend time looking at the mandala.) The pain disappeared most of the time completely.

Nevertheless, don't neglect consulting a doctor in cases of lasting problems.

The Mandalas and Their Physical and Psychological Effects

The colorful healing mandalas shown on the following pages have even greater effect when used as examples for coloring in your own therapy mandalas (see the next chapter).

In cases of serious illness, this mandala system can also be used as an adjunct to conventional treatment methods. Through its effect on the blockages at the root of the illness, it can be used to support any type of therapy. This way, lasting healing is supported on all levels.

Later, you will find indexes of physical ailments and psychological issues with references to the mandalas that are helpful for the respective problems. If several mandalas are listed, choose the one that appeals to

Note: The application of this mandala system is not a substitute for medical treatment or psychotherapy. If you have persistent physical or psychological problems, don't hesitate to get professional attention.

you the most, based on your intuitive feeling. That will be exactly the right one for you and will help you overcome your problems.

It should also be noted that, when it comes to severe conditions, the following mandalas are meant to be used in conjunction with medical treatment.

Mandala 1a

Physical Problems

Abscesses and inflammations in the head area, acute cerebral apoplexy, acute disorders in the lymphatic system, acute sinusitis, allergies, angina, bleeding of the brain, concussion of the brain, dizziness, earaches, encephalitis, epilepsy, erysipelas, extreme excitement, eye inflammations and other eye problems, fever, frontal sinus catarrh, gum inflammation, gum wounds after dental treatment, hair mycosis, hay fever, head injuries, heat stroke, heat waves, inflammation of the middle ear, inflammations and eczema of the auditory canal, inflammations of the throat, influenza, measles, meningitis, migraine, nervous headaches or headaches due to overexertion, neuralgic face pains, pain in the jaw area, periodontitis, runny nose, sleeping problems including sleeplessness, sty in the eye, throat catarrh, toothaches, and trigeminal neuralgia.

Problems and Issues on the Level of the Psyche

Aggression, agitation (increases calmness), being fixated on control, being overly responsible, being overly wound up (especially in children), egoism, excessive emotions, excessive orderliness, excessive thinking, fear, hallucinations, hysteria, intolerance, nervousness, neuroses, not being able to forgive, obsessions, poor concentration, pressure to achieve, pride, self-overestimation, sleeping problems including sleeplessness, stress, striving for dominance, and stubbornness.

Mandala 1b

Physical Problems

Cerebral apoplexy, chronic congested head colds and head colds at the beginning stage, chronic disorders in the lymphatic system, chronic earaches, chronic eye disorders without pain, chronic neck pain, chronic sinusitis, consciousness weakness, eye weakness, fatigue in the spring, hair loss, headaches due to lack of exercise, hearing problems, lack of sense of smell and sense of taste, poliomyelitis, and shock conditions.

Problems and Issues on the Level of the Psyche

Absentmindness, being too modest, depression, excessive self-sacrifice/devotion to others, forgetfulness, hopelessness, irrationality, lack of control, lack of discipline, lack of order, and mental fatigue, as well as a desire for a new beginning, greater self-assurance, increased ability in absorbing information, increased sense of responsibility, stronger powers of concentration, and the ability to think more logically.

Mandala 1c

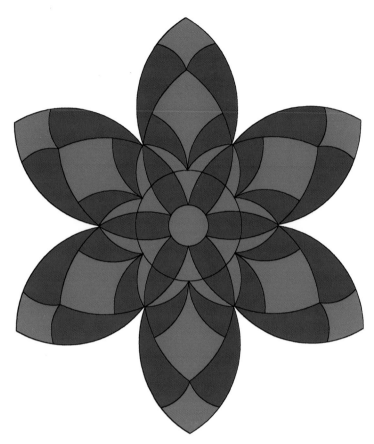

Physical Problems

Cerebral apoplexy, chronic disorders in the lymphatic system, chronic ear pain, chronic eye disorders without pain, chronic neck pain, chronic sinusitis, consciousness weakness, eye weakness, fatigue in the spring, hair loss, head colds in the beginning stage and colds with congestion, headaches due to lack of exercise, hearing problems, lack of sense of smell and taste, poliomyelitis, and shock conditions.

Problems and Issues
on the Level of the Psyche

Absentmindedness, being too modest, depression, excessive self-sacrifice/devotion to others, forgetfulness, hopelessness, irrationality, lack of discipline, and mental fatigue, as well as a desire for a new beginning, greater self-assurance, increased ability in absorbing information, increased sense of responsibility, stronger powers of concentration, and the ability to think more logically.

Mandala 2a

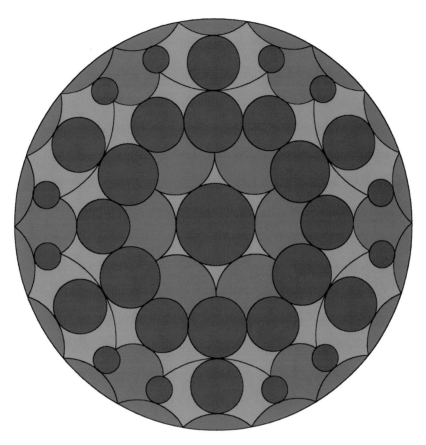

Physical Problems

Acute ear disorders, acute infectious diseases, acute jaw problems, acute lymph inflammations, acute tennis arm, allergies, angina, frontal sinus suppuration, hoarseness, inflamed tonsils, irritating cough, middle-ear inflammation, mumps, neck and throat inflammations, neck injuries, overactive thyroid gland, periodontitis, runny nose, sinusitis and inflammation of the nose, sun allergies, sweaty hands, toothaches, and trigeminal neuralgia.

Problems and Issues on the Level of the Psyche

Performance pressure, problems letting go, and stubbornness.

Mandala 2b

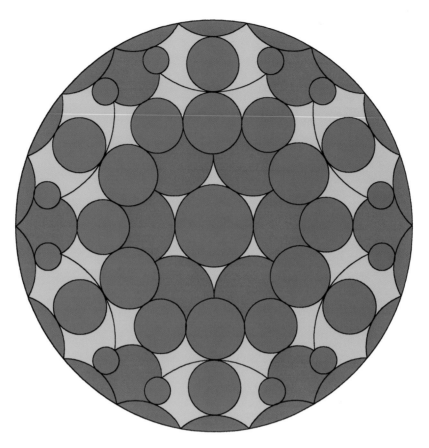

Physical Problems

Chronic disorders in the lymphatic system, chronic ear problems and pain, chronic tennis arm, cold and weak hands, diseases of the esophagus, face-nerve paralysis and pain, head colds with congestion, hearing problems, hoarseness, neck pain or stiff neck, resistance to infection, shoulder pain, subnormal functioning of the thyroid gland, teething problems in babies, and voice problems.

Problems and Issues on the Level of the Psyche

Lack of self-interest, problems accepting happiness, and the desire to enjoy life more.

Mandala 2c

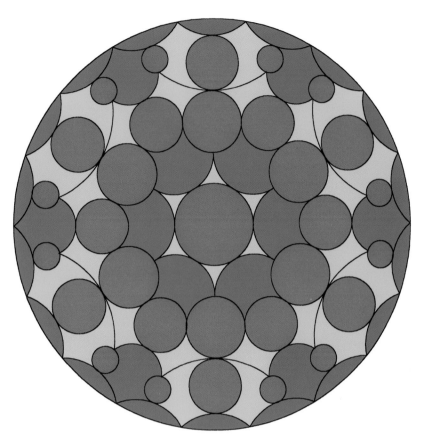

Physical Problems

Chronic disorders in the lymphatic system, chronic ear problems and pain, chronic tennis arm, cold and weak hands, diseases of the esophagus, face-nerve paralysis and pain, head colds with congestion, hearing problems, hoarseness, neck pain or stiff neck, resistance to infection, shoulder pain, subnormal functioning of the thyroid gland, teething problems in babies, and voice problems.

Problems and Issues on the Level of the Psyche

Lack of self-interest, problems accepting happiness, and the desire to enjoy life more.

Mandala 2d

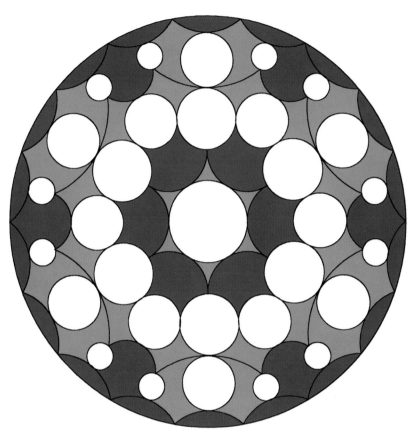

This mandala is especially effective on the level of the psyche. The so-called renunciation mandala, it is particularly helpful for people who want to raise themselves spiritually.

Applications

Avarice, exaggerated materialism, extravagance or excess in different forms, greediness for possessions, hunger or lust for power, obsessive consumption, and pride.

Mandala 3a

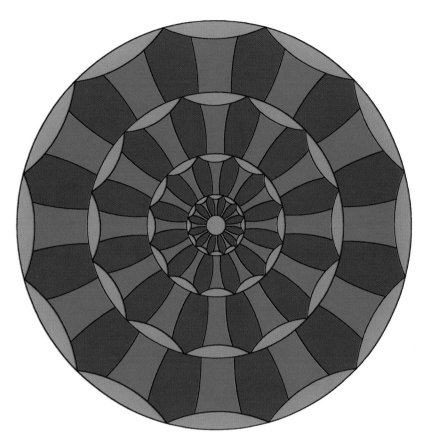

Physical Problems

Acute illnesses of the lymphatic gland, acute infectious diseases, acute muscle pain, acute tennis arm, arm pain at night, asthma, breathing difficulty, chest congestion, coughing spells, fingernail inflammation, hay fever, inflamed tonsils, lung cancer, mumps, neck and throat inflammation, pleurisy, pneumonia, poorly functioning thymus gland, sun allergies, tuberculosis, and whooping cough.

Problems and Issues on the Level of the Psyche

Foremost is the obsession with being critical.

Mandala 3b

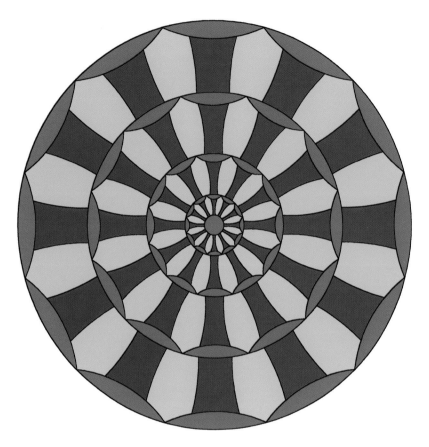

Physical Problems

Arm weakness, breathing difficulty or shortness of breath, chronic asthma, chronic disorders in the lymphatic system, chronic larynx problems, chronic lung illnesses, congestion with mucus, lack of strength in the fingers, low resistance to infection, muscle cramps, muscular pain, persistent mucus in the lungs, weak immune system, and weak muscles.

Problems and Issues on the Level of the Psyche

Aloofness, being overly reserved, difficulties in making contact, embarrassment, guilt, lack of consciousness regarding the environment, lack of social conscience, tendency to dislike people, and unsociability, as well as a desire for greater communication; also helpful in the search for a partner and in activating the neck chakra.

Mandala 4a

Physical Problems

Alcoholism, asthma, breast cancer, breast-feeding problems in mothers, breathing difficulty, chest pains, congestion with mucus in the lungs, cough, diabetes, difficulty stopping smoking, gallbladder problems, hay fever, heartburn, heat waves, high cholesterol, jaundice, liver illnesses, lung diseases, migraine, nervous eye problems, nervousness, obesity, pancreas disorders, problems with uric-acid regulation, rapid heartbeat and other heart-rhythm disorders, shingles, sleeplessness or difficulties in falling asleep, stomach ailments, vomiting, and whooping cough.

Problems and Issues on the Level of the Psyche

Anger and hatred, arrogance, anxiety (calming), being overly wound up (especially in children), claustrophobia, distrust, eating disorders, emotional wounds, fear of tests/examinations, hallucinations, hysteria, impatience, lack of sympathy or not being liberal or tolerant enough, moodiness, nervousness, pressure to achieve, problems letting go, sleeping problems including trouble falling asleep, soberness or lack of gaiety, and stress of any kind, as well as the need to restore inner balance, the wish to develop love, and the wish to further devotion.

Mandala 4b

Physical Problems

Alcoholism, asthma, breast cancer, breast-feeding problems in mothers, breathing difficulty, chest pains, congestion with mucus in the lungs, cough, diabetes, difficulty in stopping smoking, gallbladder problems, hay fever, heartburn, heat waves, high cholesterol, jaundice, liver illnesses, lung diseases, migraine, nervous eye problems, nervousness, obesity, pancreas disorders, problems with uric-acid regulation, rapid heartbeat and other heart-rhythm disorders, shingles, sleeplessness and trouble falling asleep, stomach ailments, vomiting, and whooping cough.

Problems and Issues on the Level of the Psyche

Anger and hatred, arrogance, anxiety, claustrophobia, distrust, eating disorders, emotional wounds, fear of tests/examinations, hallucinations, hysteria, impatience, lack of sympathy or not being liberal or tolerant enough, moodiness, nervousness, pressure to achieve, problems letting go, sleeping problems including trouble falling asleep, soberness or lack of gaiety, and stress of any kind, as well as the need to restore inner balance, the wish to develop love, and the wish to further devotion.

Mandala 5a

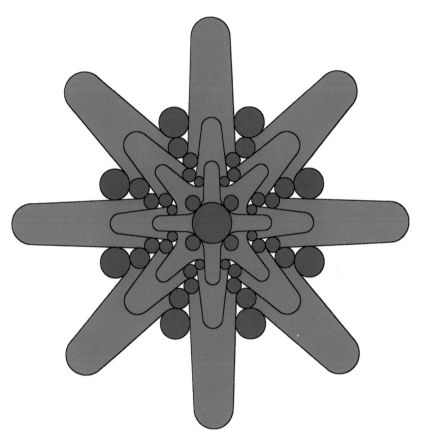

Physical Problems

Anemia, arteriosclerosis, circulation failure, convalescence, heart diseases caused by weakness, lack of iron, leukemia, low blood pressure, multiple sclerosis, overall weakness, Parkinson's disease, poor blood circulation, shivering and overly cool body temperature, sleepiness, spinal-cord weakness, and weak blood.

Problems and Issues on the Level of the Psyche

A broken heart, exhaustion, insecurity, lack of courage when it comes to the heart, lack of energy, lack of passion, learning disabilities, lethargy, and problems absorbing information, as well as a desire for greater creativity, greater self-consciousness, and increased pleasure.

Mandala 5b

Physical Problems

Acute heart diseases and ailments, difficulty stopping breast feeding, fever, heat damage, high blood pressure, inflammation of the arteries, sunstroke, thromboses, and wounds.

Problems and Issues on the Level of the Psyche

Excessive emotionality, excessive passion, hunger for power, impatience, jealousy, overstrain, rage, self-overestimation, and vanity.

Mandala 6a

Physical Problems

Bellyaches, gallbladder problems, gout, high blood sugar, liver disorders, low insulin levels, metabolic disorders, nausea, intestinal illnesses and ailments, old-age diabetes, pancreas disorders, stomach ailments, swelling of the spleen, travel sickness, and uneven appetite.

Problems and Issues on the Level of the Psyche

Doubt, eating disorders, excessive sense of duty, excessive worry, obsession with cleanliness, perfectionism, problems letting go, unreasonableness, and untidiness, plus a desire to think more logically.

Mandala 6b

Physical Problems

Acne, bloating, chronic and acute gallbladder problems, congestion, constipation, difficulty sticking to a diet, dizziness, intestinal disorders, lack of appetite, liver disorders, low blood sugar, metabolic problems, nausea, need for detoxification, shock conditions, and spleen problems.

Problems and Issues on the Level of the Psyche

Furthering the flow in all kinds of life situations and releasing blockages of feelings.

Mandala 7a

Physical Problems

Bladder stones (to aid excretion), bladder-muscle weakness, blocked urine, blood poisoning (to aid cleansing),
chronic intervertebral disc problems, chronic urinary tract
disorders, cirrhosis, disorders of the suprarenal gland,
drainage of the body, furuncles, low blood pressure, neurodermatitis, skin cancer, and swollen feet.

Mandala 7b

Physical Problems

Acute bladder problems, acute sciatica, acute skin disorders, bladder cramps, bladder infection, burns (first aid), cancer of the bladder, dry skin, herpes (skin), high blood pressure, irritated bladder, kidney colic, lumbago, pyelitis, skin anthrax, and uremia.

Mandala 8a

Physical Problems

Acute infectious abdominal diseases, ailments due to the climate, being overly stimulated sexually, night sweats, overactive functioning of the gonads, painful menstruation, and prostate cancer.

Problems and Issues
on the Level of the Psyche

Being too earthbound, being overly stimulated sexually, excessive desires, hunger for power, and lack of fidelity.

Mandala 8b

Physical Problems

Acute infectious abdominal diseases, ailments due to the climate, being overly stimulated sexually, night sweats, overactive functioning of the gonads, painful menstruation, and prostate cancer.

Problems and Issues on the Level of the Psyche

Being too earthbound, being overly stimulated sexually, excessive desires, hunger for power, and lack of fidelity.

Mandala 8c

Physical Problems

Chronic abdominal ailments caused by weakness, gonad weakness, missed or absent menstrual periods, pregnancy problems, problems with sexual potency, and uterine descent.

Problems and Issues on the Level of the Psyche

Being overly rigid and orderly, fear of intimacy, lack of connection to the earth, and lack of passion.

Mandala 8d

Physical Problems

Chronic abdominal ailments caused by weakness, gonad weakness, missed or absent menstrual periods, pregnancy problems, problems with sexual potency, and uterine descent.

Problems and Issues on the Level of the Psyche

Being overly rigid and orderly, fear of intimacy, lack of connection to the earth, and lack of passion.

Mandala 9

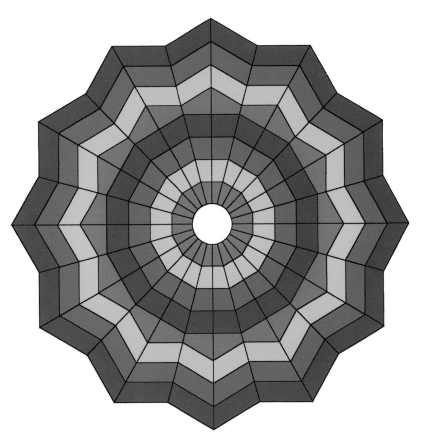

Physical Problems

Chilblains, connective-tissue weakness, inflammation in the connective tissue, rheumatism of the soft parts, upper-thigh problems, varicose veins, vein blockage, and vein inflammation.

Problems and Issues on the Level of the Psyche

The issues here all relate to change: the desire for a change, the change into a new life phase, or a new orientation.

Mandala 10a

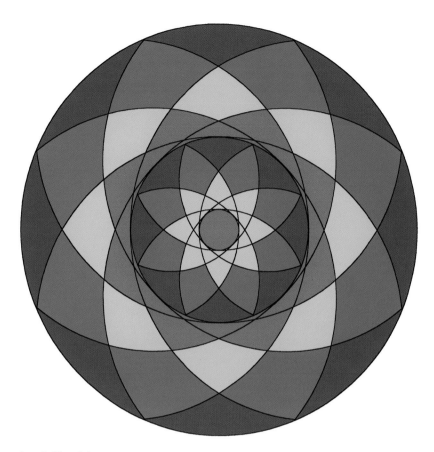

Physical Problems

Bone injuries or bone pain, calluses (helps in the formation), furuncles, gout, knee arthrosis, ligament or tendon
injuries or inflammation, meniscus injuries, old-age
ailments, pains in the joints, osteomyelitis, periostitis,
rheumatism, and skin herpes.

Problems and Issues
on the Level of the Psyche

Indecision, insecurity, and instability, as well as the desire
for greater self-confidence and the strength to actualize
things in life.

Mandala 10b

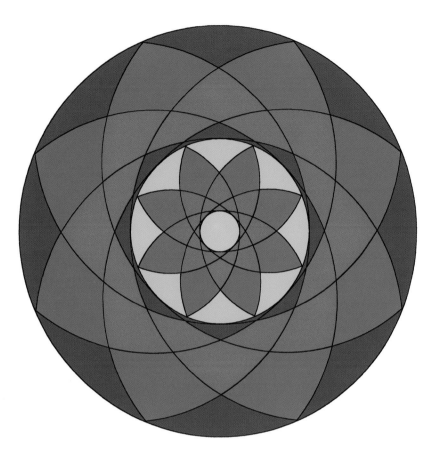

Physical Problems

Bone injuries or bone pain, calluses (helps in the formation), furuncles, gout, knee arthrosis, ligament or tendon injuries or inflammation, meniscus injuries, old-age ailments, osteomyelitis, pains in the joints, periostitis, rheumatism, and skin herpes.

Problems and Issues on the Level of the Psyche

Indecision, insecurity, and instability, as well as the desire for greater self-confidence and the strength to actualize things in life.

Mandala II

Physical Problems

Abscesses of the lower thigh, leg weakness, nerve problems, phantom pains, scars (supports the formation), thromboses (healing support), and vein disorders.

Problems and Issues
on the Level of the Psyche

Depression, difficulty in making contact with people, issues to do with the environment, lack of discernment, and panic attacks, as well as an interest in becoming more sensitive, deepening devotion, developing intuition and spirituality, furthering the visionary quest, gaining more wisdom, having a sense of greater unity, having a stronger relationship with the Divine, increasing creativity, remembering dreams better, and striving for higher things.

Mandala 12

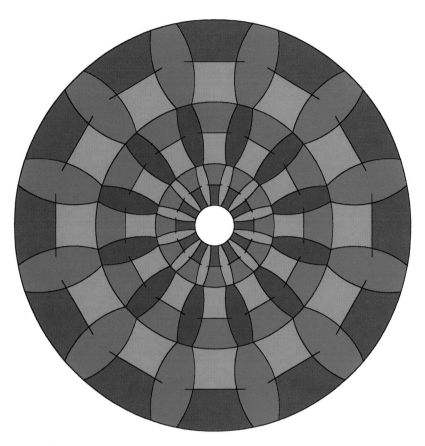

Physical Problems

Foot disorders, gland ailments, swollen feet, and toenail problems.

Problems and Issues on the Level of the Psyche

Instability, lack of discernment, plus striving for enlightenment, striving for self-realization, the search for truth, and the wish for greater inner mastery.

Weight-Loss Mandala

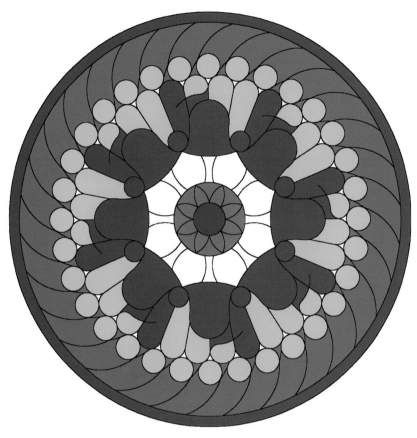

Application

A support in losing weight.

Activation Mandala I

Physical Problems

Exhaustion, fatigue in the spring, general loss of strength, heaviness in the limbs, lack of exercise, lassitude (emotional and physical), low blood pressure, multiple sclerosis, overall bodily weakness, Parkinson's disease, shivering, sleepiness, weak circulation, and weak nerves.

Problems and Issues on the Level of the Psyche

Dependency on others, depression, forgetfulness, inability to make a decision, lack of ambition, lack of courage, lack of energy, lack of motivation, laziness, powerlessness, self-pity, and weakness in thinking.

Activation Mandala 2

Physical Problems

Exhaustion, fatigue in the spring, general loss of strength, heaviness in the limbs, lack of exercise, lassitude (emotional and physical), low blood pressure, multiple sclerosis, overall bodily weakness, Parkinson's disease, shivering, sleepiness, weak circulation, and weak nerves.

Problems and Issues
on the Level of the Psyche

Dependency on others, depression, forgetfulness, inability to make a decision, lack of ambition, lack of courage, lack of energy, lack of motivation, laziness, powerlessness, self-pity, and weakness in thinking.

Counteracting-Burnout Mandala

Physical Problems

Acute heart diseases, danger of cardiac infarction, heart ailments, high blood pressure, nervous heartbeat, and stomach pain.

Problems and Issues on the Level of the Psyche

Being authoritarian, excessive emotions, excessive hunger for life, hunger for power, overstrain, overwork, stress, plus the wish to create greater camaraderie in the working environment (also helpful when the mandala is hung up on the wall at the workplace).

Balance Mandala

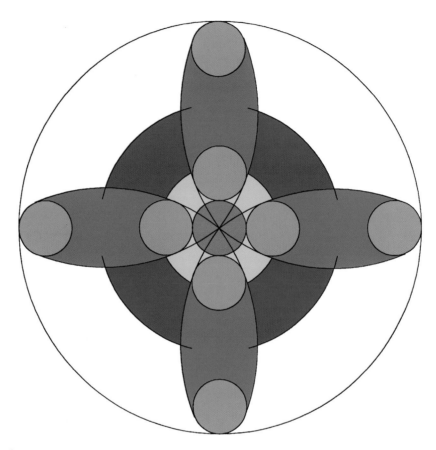

Application

This mandala is used for stabilizing or sustaining a condition already achieved from mandala therapy. With this balance mandala, yow can further anchor this newly gained condition. Then from this level you can address other problems.

Birth Mandala

Application

This mandala is used only during or shortly before child-
birth, as otherwise labor pains could get induced. Its
purpose is to harmonize the process of giving birth.

Feeling Mandala

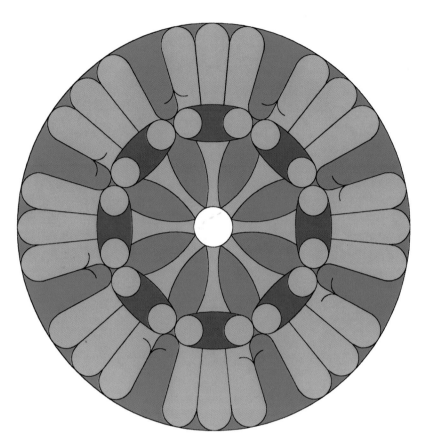

Physical Problems

Asthma and being overweight.

Problems and Issues on the Level of the Psyche

Bitterness, confusion of feelings, desire to control, dissatisfaction, egoism, excessive logic, lack of caring, lack of devotion, lack of joy, lack of love, lack of maternal qualities, overly stern opinions, and suppression of feelings.

Mandala for Cardiac Infarction or Heart Attack

Physical Problems

Acute heart diseases, cardiac infarction, heart ailments, high blood pressure, and nervous heartbeat.

Problems and Issues on the Level of the Psyche

Being authoritarian, excessive emotions, excessive hunger for life, hunger for power, and stress.

Immune-System Mandala

Applications

To prevent or support the healing of all infectious diseases
of the ear, nose, and throat area, as well as lung infections
and bacterial infections.

Intuition Mandala

Applications

Clinging to old blocking behavioral patterns, expectations
of disaster, fixation on the past, hopelessness, lack of belief
and trust, lack of creativity, lack of harmony between heart
and mind, lack of inspiration, lack of intuition, lack of
intuition especially in listening to one's own body, lack of
sensibility, lack of spiritual relationships, lack of spirituality,
and loss of emotional-spiritual values, as well as an interest
in awakening the longing for the Divine, increasing the
ability to adapt, and listening more to one's inner voice.

Psychic Healing Mandala

Physical Problems

Alcoholism, all types of cancer (in support of medical care and for harmonizing the physical processes), drug withdrawal and the physical problems that accompany it, enormous stress, mental illnesses of any kind, obsession with being thin, and total physical exhaustion.

Problems and Issues on the Level of the Psyche

Cruelty, extreme conditions of fear, extreme fear of relationships, hatred, hysteria, jealousy, mania, mental illnesses, nervous breakdown, and phobias.

Stroke Mandala

Application

Preventive and to support medical treatment.

Protection Mandala

Physical Problems

Alcoholism, all types of cancer (as support for medical care and for harmonizing the physical processes), drug addiction, obesity, obsession with being thin, overstrain, resistance to infection, and stress.

Problems and Issues on the Level of the Psyche

Alcoholism, all types of mental illness, bed-wetting in children, depression, extreme sensitivity, fears, lack of distance, lack of mental solace, neediness for protection, and nightmares.

Addiction Mandala

Applications

Physical and psychological effects of all types of addiction, including addiction to consumption, addiction to nicotine, alcoholism, compulsive eating, drug addiction, and obsession with being thin.

Willpower Mandala

Applications

Being too adaptable, being too easily influenced by others, dependency on opinions and ideas of other people, general weakness in willpower, hopelessness, lack of ambition, lack of discipline, lack of motivation, lack of perseverance, lack of self-control, laziness in thinking, overall laziness, power-lessness, and resignation; plus as support to stopping smoking.

Mandalas to Color In Yourself

First, it would be a good idea to make several Xerox copies of the black-and-white patterns on the following pages. Then, when you have recognized certain problems, all you need to do is reach for the appropriate copies and begin coloring in the shapes. Among the mandalas recommended for your specific problems in the indexes, choose the ones that appeal to you the most. Then replicate the colors in those mandalas, shown in the previous chapter, by coloring in the shapes in the corresponding black-and-white patterns.

Pattern for Mandalas 1a, 1b, and 1c

Pattern for Mandalas 2a, 2b, 2c, and 2d

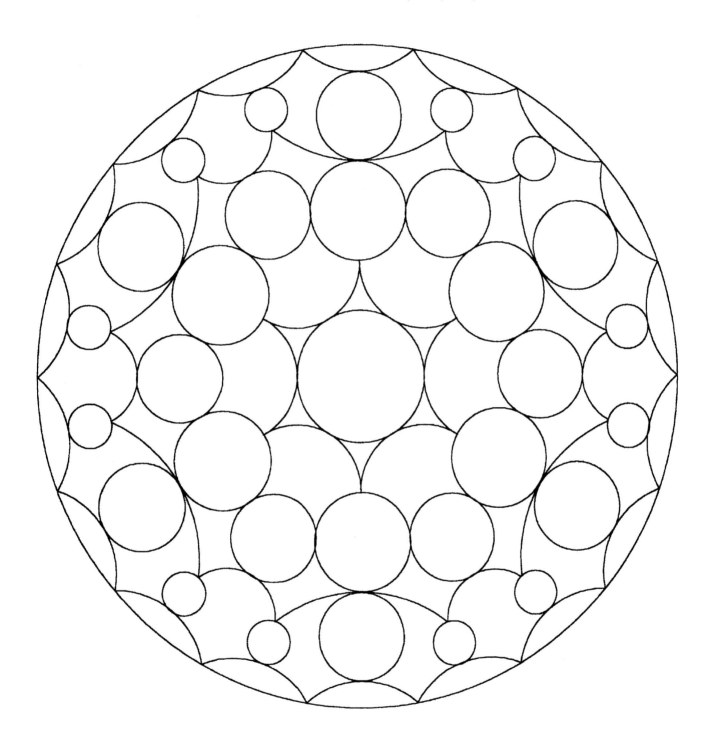

Pattern for Mandalas 3a and 3b

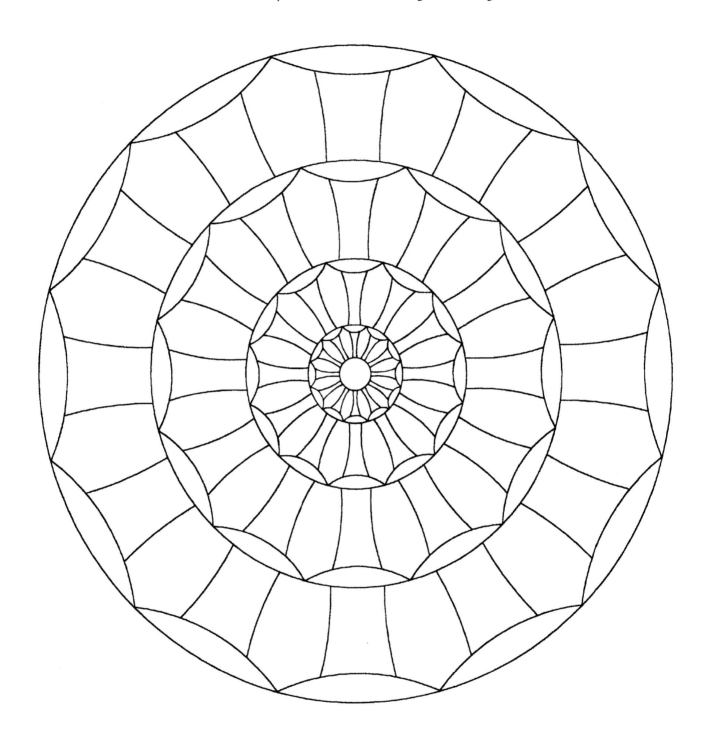

Pattern for Mandalas 4a and 4b

Pattern for Mandalas 5a and 5b

Pattern for Mandalas 6a and 6b

Pattern for Mandalas 7a and 7b

Pattern for Mandalas 8a, 8b, 8c, and 8d

Pattern for Mandala 9

Pattern for Mandalas 10a and 10b

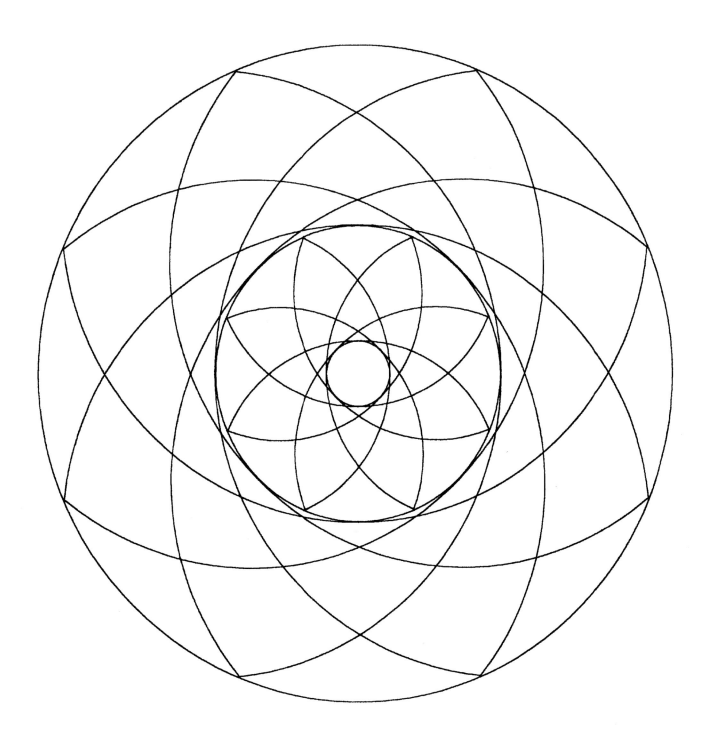

Pattern for Mandala 11

Pattern for Mandala 12

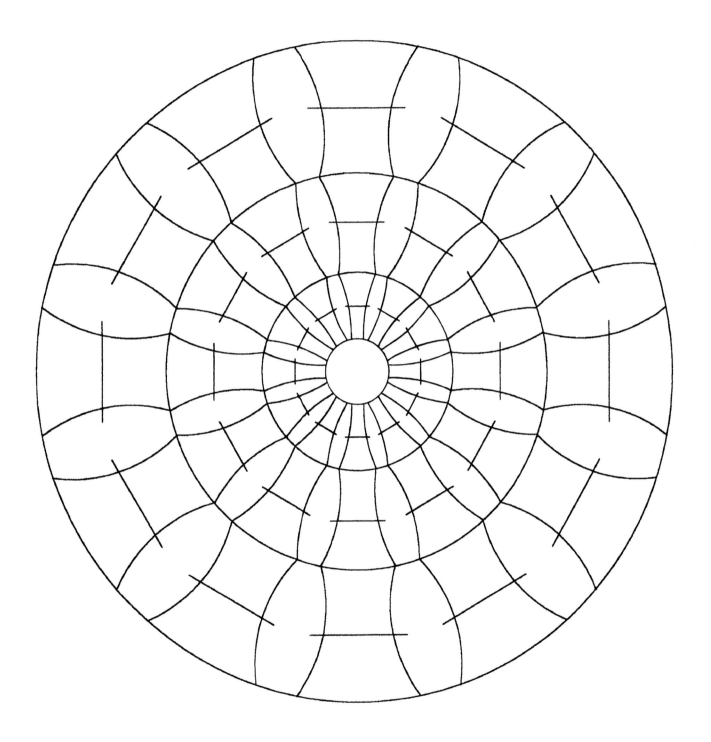

Pattern for Weight-Loss Mandala

Pattern for Activation Mandalas 1 and 2

Pattern for Counteracting-Burnout Mandala

Pattern for Balance Mandala

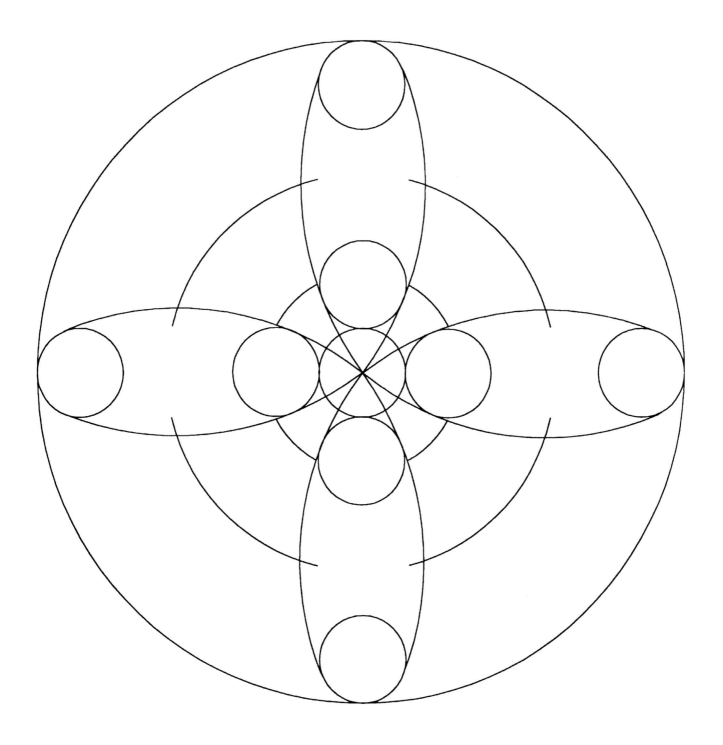

Pattern for Feeling Mandala

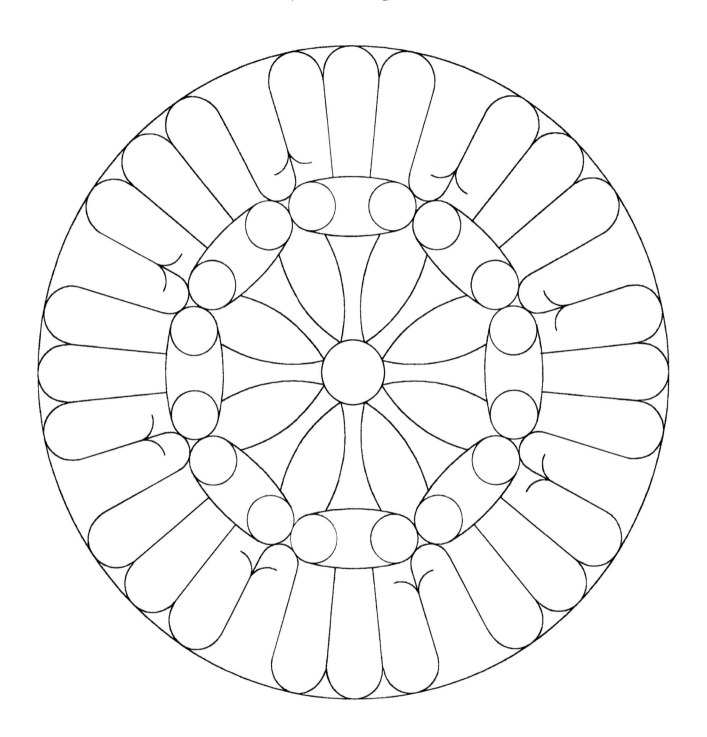

Pattern for Intuition Mandala

Pattern for Willpower Mandala

Pattern for Birth Mandala

Pattern for Heart-Attack Mandala

Pattern for Immune-System Mandala

Pattern for Psychic Healing Mandala

Pattern for Stroke Mandala

Pattern for Protection Mandala

Pattern for Addiction Mandala

Pattern for Combined Mandalas (Addiction, Birth, Heart Attack, Immune System, Protection, Psychic Healing, Stroke)

Indexes of Conditions and Their Healing Mandalas

The numbers that appear next to the physical ailments and the negative psychological conditions correspond to the mandalas that can be used to help the indicated problems. In other words, the numbers shown are the numbers of the mandalas that are effective for the respective problems. Along with these numbers, other mandalas (such as Immune-System, Activation, and Protection Mandalas) are listed by name.

If several mandalas are listed, select the one to which you are most attracted. Using precisely those colors in the respective colored mandala in the book, color in the shapes in the Xerox copy you have made of the black-and-white pattern. Or you can place the palm of your hand on the colored mandala in the book; this is a good way to go especially in cases of acute problems or pain, when you need help immediately. For chronic illnesses or psychological problems, on the other hand, it's recommended to work regularly with the respective healing mandala (at best three to five minutes daily), after you have colored in the shapes on the Xerox copy.

Index of Physical Ailments

Cystitis: 8a, 8b

Dementia praecox: 1b, Activation Mandala 2

Dental problems: 1b, 2b, 2c

Detoxification: 6b

Diabetes: 4a, 4b, 6a

Diarrhea: 6a

Diet, support for: 6b

Digestion, to foster: 6b

Digestive organs, disorders of: 6a, 6b

Diuretic: 7a

Dizziness: 1a, 4a, 6a

Dorsal vertebra injuries, to support healing of: 10a, 10b

Drainage: 7a

Dropsy: 7a

Drug addiction: Addiction Mandala, Psychic Healing Mandala, Protection Mandala

Duodenum ulcer: 4a, 6a, 6b

Dysentery: 6a, 6b

Ear diseases, acute: 1a, 2a

Ear diseases, chronic: 1b, 2b

Earaches: 1a, 2a

Ears, buzzing in: 1a, 4a

Encephalitis, healing support for: 1a

Epilepsy: 1a

Erysipelas: 1a

Esophagus disorders, acute: 2a

Esophagus disorders, chronic: 2c

Excitement, extreme: 1a, 4a, 6a

Excretion, to foster: 6a, 6b

Exhaustion (mental): Activation Mandalas 1 and 2, Psychic Healing Mandala

Exhaustion (physical): Activation Mandalas 1 and 2

Eye abscesses: 1a, 4a

Eye ailments: 1a

Eye catarrh: 1a, 4a

Eye infection: 1a

Eye injury: 1a

Eye weakness: 1b

Eye, pressure in: 1a

Eyes, burning: 1a

Eyes, strengthening of: 1b, 1c

Eyes, swimming: 1a, 4a

Face pains (neuralgia): 1a

Face-nerve paralysis: 1b, 2b

Fallopian-tube infection: 8a, 8b

Fasting, support for: 6b

Fatigue, extreme: 4a

Fatigue, in the spring: 1b, Activation Mandalas 1 and 2

Feet, cold: 12

Feet, strengthening of: 12

Feet, sweaty: 12

Feet, swollen: 12

Feet, water retention in: 7a, 12

Fever, to lower: 1a, 5b

Finger cramps: 3b

Finger weakness: 3b

Fingernail-bed infection: 3a

Fingernails, brittle: 3b

Flu: 1a, 2a

Foot disorders: 12

Foot fungus: 12

Foot pains: 12

Foot, rheumatism in: 12, 10a

Foreskin infection: 8a, 8b

Frigidity: 8c, 8d

Frontal sinus catarrh: 1a

Frontal sinus festering: 1a, 2a

Furuncle: 7a, 10a, 10b

Gallbladder blockage: 6b

Gallbladder infections: 4b, 6a

Heat waves: 5b

Hemorrhoid bleeding: 8a, 8b

Hemorrhoids: 8a, 8b

Hepatitis: 4a

Herpes: 7b

Hiccups: 4a

Hip problems: 10a, 10b

Hip-joint pains: 10a, 10b

Hoarseness, from head cold: 2b

Hoarseness, from overstrain: 2a

Hormone disorders: 12

Hyperacidity: 4a, 6a

Hysteria: 4a, Psychic Healing Mandala

Immune system, strengthening of: 2c, 3b, Protection
Mandala, Immune-System Mandala

Infections, curbing of: 1a, 4a

Infectious diseases, acute: 1a, 2a, 3a, 4a, Protection
Mandala, Immune-System Mandala

Influenza: 1a, 2a, 4a, Protection Mandala, Immune-
System Mandala

Insulin, low: 6a

Intervertebral disks, acute and chronic problems: 7a

Intestinal bleeding: 6a

Intestinal cancer: 6a, 6b, Protection Mandala, Psychic
Healing Mandala

Intestinal catarrh: 6a

Intestinal colic: 6a, 6b

Intestinal cramps: 6b

Intestinal fungus: 6b

Intestinal illness, infectious: 6a

Intestinal paralysis: 6b

Intestinal parasites: 6b

Intestinal sluggishness: 6b

Intestinal stoppage (until the doctor arrives): 6a, 4a

Intestinal ulcers: 6a

Intestine infection: 6a

Intestine, detoxification of: 6b

Intestine, strengthening of: 6b, 6a

Invigoration, need for: Activation Mandalas 1 and 2

Iris infection: 1a

Iron, lack of: 5a, 10a, 10b

Irritated bladder: 7b

Itching skin: 7b

Jaundice: 4a

Jaw infection: 2a

Joint inflammation: 10a, 10b

Joint pains: 10a, 10b

Joint rheumatism: 10a, 10b

Kidney activity, to stimulate: 7a

Kidney colic: 7b

Kidney irritation: 7b

Kidney troubles, acute: 7b

Kidney troubles, chronic: 7a

Kidneys, cleansing of: 7a

Knee arthrosis: 10a, 10b

Labor pains: 8c, 8d, Birth Mandala

Lack of blood: 5a, 9

Large-intestine infection: 6a

Laryngitis: 2a

Laryngospasm: 2c

Larynx ailments, acute: 2a

Larynx ailments, chronic: 2b, 2c

Larynx cancer: 2a, 2b, 2c, 2d, Protection Mandala,
Psychic Healing Mandala

Larynx infection: 2a

Lassitude: 10, Activation Mandala 2

Leg cramps: 9, 11

Leg injuries, healing support for: 10a, 10b

Legs, weak: 11

Leukemia: 5a, Protection Mandala, Psychic Healing
Mandala

Ligament injuries: 10, 10a, 10b

Limb heaviness: Activation Mandala 2

Limbs, hurting: 10a, 10b

Lips, acute pain: 1a

Liver atrophy: 6b

Liver blockage: 6b

Liver cancer: 4a, 6a, Protection Mandala, Psychic
　　Healing Mandala

Liver damage through toxins or medications: 6b

Liver damage, general: 6a

Liver diseases, acute: 6a, 4a

Liver disorders: 6a, 6b

Liver infection: 6a, 4a

Liver stricture: 6a, 6b

Liver, cirrhosis of: 4a, 6b

Liver, fatty: 4a

Liver, hardened: 4a, 6b

Liver, swelling of: 6a

Liver-gallbladder ailments, chronic: 6b, 4a

Lumbago: 7b, 10a, 10b

Lumbar-vertebra injuries, healing support for: 10a,
　　10b

Lung cancer: 3a, 4a, Psychic Healing Mandala,
　　Protection Mandala

Lung catarrh: 3a, 4a

Lung diseases, acute, first aid for: 3a, 4a

Lung diseases, chronic: 3b, Psychic Healing Mandala

Lungs, blocked, with mucus: 3b

Lungs, strengthening of: 3b

Lymphangitis: 1a, 2a, 3a

Lymphatic gland disorders: 1a, 2a, 3a

Lymphatic glands, swelling of: 1a, 2a, 3a

Lymphatic system disorders, acute: 1a, 2a, 3a

Lymphatic system disorders, chronic: 1b, 2b, 3b

Lymphatic vessel diseases: 1a, 2a, 3a

Lymphatic vessel infections: 1a, 2a, 3a

Malaria: 4a, 1a

Maxillary cavity, acute pain in: 1a, 2a

Maxillary cavity, festering of: 2a

Maxillary-cavity infection: 2a

Measles: 1a, 7b

Memory, strengthening of: 1b, Activation Mandala 1

Meningitis: 1a

Meniscus injury, healing support for: 10a, 10b

Menopausal ailments: 4a, 8a, 8b, Intuition Mandala,
　　Feeling Mandala

Menstrual periods, skipped or absent: 7a, 8c, 8d

Menstruation, painful: 8a, 8b

Metabolism disorders: 6a

Metabolism, to speed up: 6b, Activation Mandalas 1
　　and 2

Middle-ear infection: 1a, 2a

Migraine: 1a, 4a

Milk secretion in breastfeeding mothers, to increase:
　　4b

Mothers, nursing, support for: 4a

Mouth abscess: 1a, 2a

Mouth blisters: 1a, 2a

Mouth infection: 1a, 2a

Mouth mucous-membrane infection: 1a, 2a

Mouth, dry: 1b, 1c

Movement, to foster: Activation Mandala 2

Mucous follicle infection: 10a, 10b

Mucous membranes, bleeding of: 1a, 4a

Mucus, blocked: 4a, 3a

Mucus, to eliminate: 4b

Multiple sclerosis: 1b, 1c, 5a, Activation Mandalas 1
　　and 2, Willpower Mandala

Mumps: 1a, 2a, 3a

Muscle cramps: 3b

Muscle pains, acute: 3a

Muscle pains, caused by weakness: 3b

Muscle weakness: 3b

Muscles, strengthening of: 10a, 10b, 3b

Muscular rheumatism: 10a, 10b

Nasal catarrh: 1a

Nasal mucus membrane, dry: 1b

Nasal sinusitis, acute: 1a, 2a, Immune-System Mandala

Nasal sinusitis, chronic: 1b, 2b, Immune-System Mandala

Nausea: 4a, 6a

Neck injuries, first aid for: 2a, 3a

Neck muscles, to activate: 2b

Neck pains: 1b, 2b

Nephritis: 7b

Nerves, to strengthen: 1b, 4a, Activation Mandala 1, Willpower Mandala, Protection Mandala

Nervous debility: 11, Psychic Healing Mandala

Nervous disorders: 11

Nervous irritation: 1a, 11

Nervous unrest: 4a, Burnout-Counteracting Mandala, Psychic Healing Mandala

Nervousness: 1a, 4a, 11

Neuralgia: 4a, 11

Neuralgic pain: 1a, 11

Neuritis: 1a, 11

Neurodermatitis: 7a, 10a, 10b

Night sweats: 8a, 8b

Nose, broken, first aid for: 1a

Nose, runny: 1a, 2a, Immune-System Mandala

Nose, stuffed: 1b

Nosebleed: 1a, 4a

Obesity: 4b, 6a, 6b, Feeling Mandala, Protection Mandala

Obsession with being thin: 4a, Psychic Healing Mandala, Protection Mandala, Addiction Mandala

Old-age ailments: 10a, 10b

Old-age diabetes: 4b, 6a

Optic-nerve inflammation: 1a

Osteomyelitis: 10a, 10b

Ovary infection: 8a, 8b

Overactive functioning of the gonads: 8a, 8b

Overstrain: 1a, 4a, Burnout-Counteracting Mandala, Protection Mandala

Overweight: 4a, Weight-Loss Mandala, Protection Mandala

Pains, phantom: 11, 4a, Protection Mandala, Psychic Healing Mandala

Pancreas disorders: 4a, 6a, 6b

Pancreatitis: 4a, 6a

Paralysis: 12

Parkinson's disease: 10a, 10b, 5a, Activation Mandalas 1 and 2

Pelvis, broken, healing support for: 10a, 10b

Pericardium infection: 5b

Periodontitis: 1a, 2a

Periostitis: 10a, 10b

Perspiration, increased, to control: 4a

Perspiration, to increase: 5a

Phlegmons: 2b, 3b

Physical abilities, loss of: Activation Mandala, Willpower Mandala

Pimples, to foster cleansing of: 1b

Pleuralgia: 4a, 5b

Pleurisy: 2a, 3a

Pneumonia: 3a, 4a

Poisoning: 6a

Poliomyelitis, spinal: 1b, Activation Mandala 2

Pregnancy problems: 8c, 8d

Pregnancy, until shortly before birth: 4a, Protection Mandala, Feeling Mandala

Prostate cancer: Protection Mandala, Psychic Healing Mandala

Urinary-passage infection: 8a, 8b

Urinary-tract diseases, acute: 8a, 8b

Urinary-tract diseases, chronic: 8c, 8d, 7a

Urinary-tract infection, acute: 8a, 8b, 7b

Urination, involuntary: 7a, 8c, 8d

Urination, painful: 7b, 8a, 8b

Urine blockage, to foster excretion: 7a

Urine retention: 7a

Urine, albumin in: 8a

Urine, passing blood in: 8a, 8b, 7b

Uterine cancer: Protection Mandala, Psychic Healing Mandala

Uterus bands, weak: 8c, 8d

Uterus bleeding: 8a, 8b

Uterus cramps: 8c, 8d

Uterus descent: 8c, 8d

Uterus infection: 8a, 8b

Uterus weakness: 8c, 8d

Vaginal infections: 8a, 8b

Varicose veins: 9, 11

Vein blockage: 9, 11

Vein disorders: 11

Vein hardening: 5a

Vein infection: 9, 11

Vein infections, external (skin): 1a

Vocal-cord paralysis: 2c

Voice, rough: 2c

Vomiting: 4a

Warts: 4a, 6a

Waste, to eliminate: 6b

Water retention: 7b

Weakness of the body, general: 5a, Activation Mandalas 1 and 2

Weather sensitivity: 4a

Weight gain, support for: 4b

Weight loss, pathological: 6a

Weight loss, support for: Willpower Mandala, Weight-Loss Mandala

Weight, low: 4a, 6a

Weight-loss diet, support for: 6b

Whooping cough: 3a, 4a

Windpipe catarrh: 2a, 3a

Women's ailments, acute: 8a, 8b

Worms: 6a, 6b

Wounds, fresh: 5b, 1a

Wounds, healing support for: 11

Wounds, poorly healing: 5a

Index of Problems and Issues on the Level of the Psyche

Absentmindedness: 1b, 1c, Activation Mandalas 1 and 2

Absorbing information, problem in: 1b, 1c, 5a, Activation Mandalas 1 and 2

Achievement pressure: 1a, 2a, 4a

Achievement, lack of: Activation Mandalas 1 and 2, Willpower Mandala

Activity, to foster: Activation Mandalas 1 and 2

Adaptability, excessive: Willpower Mandala

Adaptability, to foster: Intuition Mandala, Feeling Mandala

Addictive behavior: Addiction Mandala, Protection Mandala, Psychic Healing Mandala

Aggressions: 1a, 4a

Alcoholism: Addiction Mandala, Protection Mandala, Psychic Healing Mandala

Ambition, lack of: Willpower Mandalas 1–3, Activation Mandalas 1 and 2

Anxiety: 5a, Willpower Mandala

Authoritarianism: 1a, 4a, Heart-Attack Mandala, Psychic Healing Mandala

Avarice: 2d, 4

Balance, inner, to establish: 4a

Balance, to establish in feeling and thinking: Intuition Mandala

Bed-wetting: Protection Mandala, Psychic Healing Mandala

Beginning of school, help in: 11, Activation Mandala 1 and 2, Willpower Mandala

Beginning, new, need for: 1b

Bipolar illness: Addiction Mandala, Psychic Healing Mandala, Protection Mandala

Bitterness: 1a, 4a, Feeling Mandala

Blocked, being: 1a, 11, Intuition Mandala

Boundaries, lack of: Protection Mandala

Boundaries, to foster: Protection Mandala

Boundaries, too strict: Feeling Mandala

Calm, wish for: 4a, Protection Mandala

Care, lack of: Feeling Mandala, Intuition Mandala

Change into a new life phase, adjustment to: 9, 11, Intuition Mandala

Change, ability to, fostering: 9

Change, wish for: 9, 11, Intuition Mandala

Charisma, lack of: Activation Mandalas 1 and 2

Cheerfulness, to achieve: 4a, 5a

Child, inner, to work with: 11, Intuition Mandala

Clarity of goals, to achieve: 9, Intuition Mandala

Claustrophobia: 4a, Psychic Healing Mandala

Cleanliness, excessive need for: 6a

Clumsiness: 5a, Activation Mandala

Cold feelings: 4a, 9, Feeling Mandala

Comfort, need for: 4a

Communication, to increase: 3b

Compulsive behavior: 1a, 11

Concentration, poor: 1a

Concentration, to increase: 1b, 1c

Confusion: 1c

Connection to other people, need to establish: 11, Intuition Mandala

Consolation of the soul: Intuition Mandala, Protection Mandala

Consumption addiction: 2d

Contact with others, difficulties in: 3b, 3c, 11

Control fixation: 1a, Feeling Mandala, Intuition Mandala

Control, lack of: 1b, 11, Willpower Mandala

Courage, lack of: 5a, Activation Mandalas 1 and 2, Willpower Mandala

Courage, to develop: 5a, Willpower Mandala

Cowardice: Willpower Mandalas 1–3

Creativity, lack of: 5a, 11, Intuition Mandala

Critical, being overly: 3a

Cynicism: 1, 4a

Darkness, fear of: Protection Mandala, Psychic Healing Mandala

Daydreaming, to reduce: 1b, 5a, Activation Mandala 1, Willpower Mandala

Decisions, inability to make: Activation Mandalas 1 and 2, Willpower Mandalas 1–3

Decisive, overly, being: Intuition Mandala

Decisiveness, lack of: Willpower Mandala

Decisiveness, to foster: Activation Mandalas 1 and 2, Willpower Mandalas 1–3

Defenselessness: 1b, 5a, Willpower Mandala, Activation Mandalas 1 and 2

Dependency on opinions of others, too high: Willpower Mandala

Dependency on others, too high: Activation Mandalas 1 and 2, Willpower Mandala

Depression: 11, Psychic Healing Mandala, Protection Mandala, Activation Mandalas 1 and 2, Willpower Mandala

Desire, need to control: 8a, 8b

Desperation: 1b, 1c, Intuition Mandala

Destiny, acceptance of: Intuition Mandala

Devotion, to increase: 4a, 11, Feeling Mandala

Devotion, too much: 5a, 1b

Discipline, lack of: Willpower Mandala, Activation Mandalas 1 and 2

Dissatisfaction: 4a, Feeling Mandala

Distrust: 4a, 11

Divorce situation: 4a, Intuition Mandala, Protection Mandala

Dominance, striving for: 1a, 2d, Feeling Mandala, Intuition Mandala

Doubts, obsession with: 1a, 4a

Dreams, to have more insightful: 11, Intuition Mandala

Duty, sense of, excessive: 6a

Duty, sense of, lack of: 1b

Earth, lack of connection to: 8c, 8d, Protection Mandala

Earth, too strong connection to: 8a, 8b, 12, Intuition Mandala

Eating disorders: 4a, 6a

Egoism: 1a, 4a, Intuition Mandala, Feeling Mandala

Embarrassment: 3b, 11

Emotional healing, need for: 4a, 11

Emotional imbalance: Intuition Mandala

Emotionality, excessive: 1a, 4a, 5b, Feeling Mandala

Emotions, deep, desire for: 11

Emotions, suppressed: 11, 4a, 5b, Feeling Mandala

Empathy, expression of, to foster: Feeling Mandala

Energy, lack of: 5a, Activation Mandalas 1 and 2

Enjoyment, lack of: 2c, 2b

Enlightenment, striving for: 11, 12, Intuition Mandala

Environmental consciousness, to strengthen: 3b, 3c, 11

Exhaustion: 5a, Activation Mandalas 1 and 2

Expectation of disaster, to change: Intuition Mandalas 1–3

Extroverted, being overly: 4a, 11

Exuberance, too strong: 4a, 5b

Eye blinking, nervous: 1a, 4a

Faith, lack of: 11, Intuition Mandala

Faithfulness/loyalty, lack of: 8a, 8b, 11, Intuition Mandala

Falling asleep, problem in: 4a

Fatigue: 1b, 5a, Activation Mandalas 1 and 2

Fear of darkness: Protection Mandala, Psychic Healing Mandala

Fear of examinations: 4a, Psychic Healing Mandala

Fear of relationships: Activation Mandalas 1 and 2, Willpower Mandala

Fear of traveling: 6a

Fear, chronic: Psychic Healing Mandala, Protection Mandala

Fear: 1a, 4a, Psychic Healing Mandala

Feeling, lack of: 1, 2, 4, Feeling Mandala

Feeling, suppression of: 4a, Feeling Mandala

Feelings, confusion of: 1, 2, 4a, Feeling Mandala

Fickleness: 10a, 10b

Forcefulness: 1a, 11

Forget, being able to (dealing with the past): 4a, 6a, Intuition Mandala

Forgetfulness: 1b, Activation Mandalas 1 and 2

Forgiveness, to foster: 1a, 11

Fussiness: 1a, 4a, Intuition Mandala

Gentleness, wish for: 4a

Greed to possess: 2d

Guilt feelings: 3b, 3c, 5a

Habits, old, clinging to: Intuition Mandala, 11

Hallucinations: 1a, 4a

Happiness/good fortune, striving for: 2b, 2c, 4a, 11, Intuition Mandala

Happiness/good fortune, accepting: 2b, 2c, 4a

Harmony of feelings, to establish: 4a, Feeling Mandala

Harmony, striving for: 4a, 11

Hate: 1a, 4a, Psychic Healing Mandala

Hatred, self-: 1a, 4a, Psychic Healing Mandala

Healing, general, need for: 11, 26, Psychic Healing Mandala

Heart and spirit connection, lack of: 11, Intuition Mandala

Heart, broken: 1a, 5a, Intuition Mandala, Feeling Mandala

Heedlessness: 1b, 1c

Hopelessness: 1b, 5a, Willpower Mandala, Intuition Mandala

Humanity, love of, to foster: 4a, 11, Feeling Mandala

Humor, no sense of: 5a, 4a

Hunger for life, excessive: 3d, 5b, 5c

Hypersensitivity: Protection Mandala, Psychic-Healing Mandala

Hysteria: 4a, 1a, Psychic Healing Mandala

Idealism, wish for greater: 11, Intuition Mandala

Imbalance: 4a, 11, Intuition Mandala

Immobility: Activation Mandalas 1 and 2

Impatience: 1a, 4a

Impulsiveness: 8a, 8b

Inadequacy: Willpower Mandala, Activation Mandalas 1 and 2

Indecision: 1b, 5a, Activation Mandala, Willpower Mandala

Indifference: 6a, Activation Mandala

Inferiority complex: 5a, Psychic Healing Mandala

Infertility: 8c, 8d

Influenced too easily, being: Willpower Mandala

Inhibition in dealing with people: 3b, 3c

Inhumanity: 11, Psychic Healing Mandala

Insecurity: 1b, 10a, 10b, Willpower Mandala

Inspiration, lack of: 11, Intuition Mandala

Instability: 4a, 10a, 10b, 12

Intensity, lack of: 5a, Activation Mandalas 1 and 2

Intention, to strengthen: Willpower Mandala

Intimacy, fear of: 8c, 8d

Intolerance: 1a, 4a, 11

Intuitive ability, to foster: 11, Intuition Mandala

Irrationality: 1b

Irresponsible, being: 1b, 1c

Irritability: 1a, 4a

Jealousy: 4a, Psychic Healing Mandala

Lack of motivation: 5a, Activation Mandalas 1 and 2, Willpower Mandala

Laziness: Activation Mandalas 1 and 2, Willpower Mandalas 1–3

Leadership, fear of: 5a, 11

Learning disabilities: 1b, 5a, Activation Mandala

Learning, to foster ability in: 1b, 5a, Activation Mandala

Lethargy: 5a, Activation Mandalas 1 and 2

Letting go, to foster: 2a, 4a, 6a

Life lessons, lacking willingness to accept: 11, Intuition Mandala

Lightness, need for: 4a, 11

Listlessness: 5a, Activation Mandalas 1 and 2, Willpower Mandala

Logic, excessive: 1a, 4a, Feeling Mandala, Intuition Mandala

Logic, to increase: 1b, 6a

Love, lack of: 4a, Feeling Mandala

Love, to foster: Feeling Mandala

Luck, lack of: 2b, 2c, 5a, 11, Intuition Mandala

Mania: Addiction Mandala, Psychic Healing Mandala, Protection Mandala

Manic-depressive illness: Addiction Mandala, Psychic Healing Mandala, Protection Mandala

Masculinity, too strong: 1a, 8a, 8b

Mastery, internal, to foster: 9, 11, 12

Materialism, excessive: 2d

Maternal qualities, lack of: Feeling Mandala, Intuition Mandala

Maturity, striving for: 11

Melancholy: 1b, Activation Mandalas 1 and 2, Willpower Mandala

Mental healing, need for: 11, Intuition Mandala, Psychic Healing Mandala

Mental imbalance: Intuition Mandala

Mental laziness: 1b, Willpower Mandala, Activation Mandala 1

Moderation, lack of: 2d, Addiction Mandala

Modesty, lack of: 4a, 1a, Feeling Mandala, Intuition Mandala

Modesty, too much: 1b, 1c, Activation Mandalas 1 and 2

Moodiness: 4a

Motivation, lack of: Activation Mandalas 1 and 2, Willpower Mandala

Nail biting, nervous: 1a, 4a

Naivete: 3b, 3c

Neck chakra, to activate: 3b

Neglect, self-: Willpower Mandala

Nervous breakdown: 1a, Psychic Healing Mandala, Protection Mandala, Burnout-Counteracting Mandala

Nervousness: 1a, 4a

Neuroses: 1a, 4a, Psychic Healing Mandala

Nightmares: 4a, Protection Mandala

Nutrition, healthy, to foster: 6a

Obstinacy: 1a, 4a

Opinion of oneself, too high: 1a, 4a, 5b

Opinions, too rigid: Feeling Mandala, Intuition
Mandala

Optimism, to foster: 5a, Activation Mandalas 1 and
2, Willpower Mandala

Order, lack of: 1b

Orderliness, excessive: 1a

Outdated opinions, having: 11, Intuition Mandala

Overstrain: 1a, 4a, 5b, Burnout-Counteracting
Mandala, Heart-Attack Mandala

Overwork: 1a, 4a, 5b, Burnout-Counteracting
Mandala, Heart-Attack Mandala

Panic: 1a, 4a, Protection Mandala, Psychic Healing
Mandala

Panic attacks: 11, Protection Mandala

Parenthood, preparation for: Birth Mandala,
Intuition Mandala

Partner, search for, help in: 3b, 11, Intuition
Mandala

Passion, lack of: 5a, 8c, 8d

Passion, too much: 5b, 8a, 8b

Past, fixation on: 4a, 6a, Intuition Mandala

Path, finding, or to orient oneself anew: 9, 11,
Intuition Mandala

Patience, to foster: 4a, 5b

People, loathing for: 3b, 11

Perfection, obsession with: 6a, 6b

Perfectionism: 1a, 4a, Intuition Mandala

Perseverance, lack of: Willpower Mandala,
Activation Mandalas 1 and 2

Pessimism: 1b, 5a, Activation Mandala

Physical healing, need for: 11, Intuition Mandala

Planning, to foster: 1b, 1c

Play, inability to: 5a, Feeling Mandala

Pleasure, to activate: 5a, Feeling Mandala

Precise, being too: 1a

Pressure to achieve: 1a, 2a, 4a

Pride: 4a, 2d

Protection, search for: Protection Mandala

Purity: 6a

Rage: 1a, 4a, 5b

Reality, loss of: 1b, 4a, 5a, Protection Mandala

Relationship to God, or higher power, to
strengthen: 11, Intuition Mandala

Relationships, fear of: Activation Mandalas 1 and 2,
Willpower Mandala

Relationships, to deal more harmoniously with: 11

Relationships, wish for: 3c, Activation Mandalas 1
and 2

Reserve: 3b, 3c

Resignation: 1b, Willpower Mandala, Activation
Mandalas 1 and 2

Responsibility, lack of: 1b, 1c

Responsibility, too much: 1a

Rootless, feeling: 12, 10a, 10b

Sadness: 4a

Satisfaction, longing for: 4a, Feeling Mandala,
Intuition Mandala

Schizophrenia: Protection Mandala, Psychic
Healing Mandala

School stress: 1a, 4a

Seclusion, too much: 1b, 3b, 3c

Self-assertiveness, to foster: 5a, Activation Mandalas
1 and 2, Willpower Mandala

Self-composed, being overly: 8c, 8d, Activation
Mandalas 1 and 2

Self-confidence, to foster: 5a, 10a, 10b, Activation
Mandalas 1 and 2, Willpower Mandala

Self-control: 1b, Willpower Mandala

Self-doubt: 1b, 5a, Intuition Mandala

Self-interest, lack of: 2c, 2b, Willpower Mandala

Selfishness, extreme: 1a, 2d, Feeling Mandala,
Intuition Mandala

General Index